SPI
EGE
L&G
RAU

THE
THIRD WAVE

THE
THIRD WAVE

A Volunteer Story

ALISON THOMPSON
WITH MEIMEI FOX

SPIEGEL & GRAU

NEW YORK

2011

The Third Wave is a work of nonfiction. Some names and identifying details
have been changed.

Copyright © 2011 by Alison Thompson

Published in the United States by Spiegel & Grau, an imprint of The Random
House Publishing Group, a division of Random House, Inc., New York.

SPIEGEL & GRAU and Design is a registered trademark of Random House, Inc.

Photos on the title page and on page 73 courtesy of Juliet Coombe.
All other photos courtesy of the author.

Library of Congress Cataloging-in-Publication Data
Thompson, Alison
The third wave : a volunteer story / Alison Thompson with MeiMei Fox.
p. cm.
ISBN 978-0-385-52916-7
eBook ISBN 978-0-679-60492-1
1. Disaster relief. 2. Volunteers. I. Fox, MeiMei. II. Title.
HV553.T46 2011
974.7'1044092—dc22 2010040767

Printed in the United States of America on acid-free paper

www.spiegelandgrau.com

2 4 6 8 9 7 5 3 1

First Edition

Book design by Diane Hobbing

Dedicated to Maria Bello, Sean Penn, and Mother Teresa

My secret heroes:

Lisa Fox is my rock and tirelessly helps raise money or
goods and offers up her contacts and friends to
support me on the ground. I love you, "sista."

Jeffrey Tarrant, a quiet hero who helps endless organizations
and me with donations to support our causes. He and
his wife, Connie, have huge, kind hearts.

Mark Axelowitz, a great volunteer, friend, and supporter
of my missions. He has a deep thirst for helping
others and my life is enhanced with him in it.

ACT I
GROUND ZERO

CHAPTER 1

My Rollerblades squeaked as I sprinted through yet another set of red lights. I had come five miles but still had two more to go. Over my back hung a bag containing a hefty first aid kit, my old 8mm camera, and a small bottle of Chanel No. 5.

I quickly glanced at the sidewalks filled with people gathered around radios and television sets dragged outside from corner stores, and I picked up speed. As I got closer to my destination, I had to battle my way through crowds of people streaming in the opposite direction. Although they walked in an orderly, quiet fashion, their hair and clothes were covered in white soot, and they held on to one another like invalids. They looked like the victims of the nuclear explosion in Hiroshima, whose black-and-white photos I'd seen in books. There was no color anywhere. People all seemed to be holding cellphones to their ears but none of them were speaking. They were in shock. I turned onto the cobblestone streets, which were less crowded though more difficult to navigate on skates, and continued to make my way to the

World Trade Center. Soon, I found myself alone in a blizzard of ash and smoke that burned my eyes and throat.

Inside the cloud, I found a Latino man in his late forties dressed in an expensive blue business suit, lying unconscious on the ground. I loosened his Gucci tie and tilted his chin back to start giving him CPR, all the while calling out into the fog for help. What felt like hours later but was probably only minutes, two EMS workers ran over and carried him away.

Deeper into the smoke, I saw an arm elegantly pointing out of the rubble toward me. I began ripping at the chunks of cement, reaching in to yank the person free. When I pulled on it, only the arm came with me—there wasn't a body attached. I screamed in horror and threw it on the ground. When I looked down at it, I saw a ring with small sapphires and diamonds on the delicate wedding finger.

Still wobbling on my skates, I looked at my worst nightmare. A million pieces of paper danced around in the air currents like oversized confetti. I caught one and read someone's private bank statement, then tucked it in my backpack. The air smelled of burned plastic. There was almost no sound except for tiny beeping noises coming from underneath the rubble at regular intervals and an occasional thud on the ground. I later found out that the thuds were the sounds of people who had jumped from the skyscraper crashing to earth, and the beeps were the sounds of the alarms embedded in the uniforms of the recently buried firemen. My heart was beating louder than rain, yet I felt compelled to push farther into the darkness.

It was 10:27 a.m. on September 11, 2001, and something even bigger was about to happen.

I felt the ground moving beneath me and looked up to see the World Trade Center's nearby north tower tumbling toward me like a stack of cards. I sprinted away, frantically attempting to out-skate the avalanche that was trying to eat me alive, but then gave up and dove under a parked UPS truck.

Twenty bucket-loads of prayers later, I crawled out into the now even denser fog of sooty darkness. I saw pieces of bodies scattered about like roadkill and collected them into a pile. I counted five legs, three arms, two torsos, and half a head. All the other stuff was unrecognizable. Inside a computer monitor I saw someone's charred skull.

I found some trash bags in a destroyed shop nearby. Even though I had worked for eight years as a nurse's aide in my mother's hospital when I was a teenager and in my early twenties, I had always been squeamish at the sight of blood. I felt queasy as I stuffed the torn flesh into the bags. My thoughts froze and my nose wrinkled up as I readied myself to perform the task at hand.

Then I remembered what I'd placed in my bag at the last minute, and took out my precious bottle of Chanel No. 5 perfume. I dabbed a little bit under my nose to mask the smell of burned bodies, and it worked. I continued shuffling around like an astronaut on my first moon landing, looking for more signs of life.

Staring into the raging fires in the surrounding buildings, I thought about my friend Jonathon Connors, who worked on the 104th floor of the World Trade Center at Cantor Fitzgerald. I prayed he had gotten out. He was a good friend who worked hard to provide for his children and his wife, who had been living with a life-threatening disease. He had always secretly wanted to be an actor, so he had invested in my first film, and to thank him I'd chosen him as an extra in one of the scenes. He had been very supportive of my career and always visited me on set.

With Jonathon in mind, I pulled my old 8mm camera out of my backpack and started shooting quick, shaky images. The clicking noise of the worn film canister disturbed me. I suddenly felt guilty taking images, so I threw the camera back into my pack. I felt that if someone saw me capturing pictures of this horrific event, they would think it was a shameful thing to do. I suppressed my filmmaker instincts and didn't shoot anymore the entire time I was on-site at Ground Zero.

When I ran across survivors, they walked past me with blank stares on their faces like zombies in a silent horror movie. Occasionally I stumbled upon other ordinary folks doing what I was doing—trying desperately to find people still alive among the wreckage and ripping down the wood pylons that were mounted on surrounding buildings to create makeshift stretchers for the injured.

An hour later, policemen started screaming for everyone to move away from the World Trade Center area. Reluctantly, I obeyed their commands, but I knew I wasn't done yet.

It became too difficult to navigate on skates, but in my mad rush to get to the disaster area as quickly as possible, I had forgotten to pack shoes. So I left my Rollerblades beside the Stuyvesant School wall just off the West Side Highway and quickly walked in my socks to a nearby pet store. In a Schwarzenegger-movie moment of grandiosity, I announced in my most assertive voice, "I am a nurse and I have no shoes. I need to go in and help people, so I need your shoes now!" The stunned Asian man at the checkout counter balked at first, throwing me a suspicious look. He then revealed his feet, probably hoping I'd pass on the thin, open-toed flaps of plastic he wore. But they were good enough for me. I took his business card, confiscated his flip-flops, and told him I'd be back.

The officials had us gather at the City Hall Park, located a few blocks northeast of Ground Zero. Shocked civilians continued to wander the streets with vacant expressions on their faces, but a gang of eager volunteers like me fought for information about how we could help. A tough guy on a bullhorn took control, asking if anyone had any medical or Army experience. I raised my hand. I didn't know what we'd be doing, but I knew I could help somehow. He and a few other construction worker–type men sorted us into groups. I joined the medical group.

A few hours later, we loaded into a New York City public bus now manned by a policeman and headed back over to the West Side Highway. Those five long blocks resembled a ghost town. It was surreal to think how busy the streets would have been just hours before. The scenery passed by in slow motion, as though time itself were snoozing. I watched five Hasidic men running toward Ground Zero with boxes of bottled water on their heads. I looked up and saw a shirtless man sitting on his window ledge, smoking a cigarette and surveying his demolished neighborhood.

The West Side Highway was full of firefighters and ambulances. As we drove closer to the World Trade Center area, I saw that the fallen towers had completely buried the highway. Everything was covered in white dust, like winter's first snowfall.

We exited the buses and regrouped in a nearby building. The local hospitals had already donated large boxes of medical supplies, so we packed our backpacks and grabbed as many bags of saline as we could carry.

I saw a large man standing near a swarm of firefighters about one block north of Ground Zero. He introduced himself to me as

Michael Voudoras. He was a volunteer EMT who had ropes and a huge medical kit slung over his sturdy back and a wild, confident look in his eyes. I knew at once that we were going to get along.

At 5:30 p.m., World Trade Center Tower Seven collapsed. I had been watching it burn since the morning and was just one block away when I found myself running for cover for the second time that day. By then, the fires were burning freely and the crazy air was filled with wind and ash.

After that, the officials cleared us out once more and announced that *nobody* would be allowed back into the Ground Zero area, since they thought many more buildings would collapse. They moved us back out and blocked off road access. All the rescue workers were frustrated, and Michael and I started getting antsy just standing around feeling helpless. A cranky nurse in scrubs declared that she was going into Ground Zero anyway, and marched off down the street, only to be stopped by storm troopers.

It was starting to get dark when a slick black car with four men inside pulled up to our area. It looked like a scene out of the movie *Men in Black*. A mysterious suit-clad arm emerged from behind the tinted windows and placed a loudspeaker on the car's roof. Earlier, someone had placed a spotlight on the ground to light up the area after nightfall, and it shone through the car, making the shadowy figures inside look even more impressive. A radio broadcast began. It was President George W. Bush telling us that we were now at war. The crowd was spellbound. Hundreds of rescue workers surrounded the car, hanging on every word. Then, just as quickly as it had appeared, the car quietly vanished. A buzz of excitement hissed through the crowd. I felt a surge of pride: We were now soldiers, fighting on American soil.

At this stage, only a small group of exhausted firemen were being allowed back into Ground Zero. But who was going to take care of the firefighters, I wondered? Michael and I gave each other a cheeky look and then hid behind a group of firemen, using them as cover to sneak back into the danger zone. We knew that many firemen were still getting hurt, and we were determined to help them. We were also eager to look around for anyone who had been buried alive.

As we stepped into the ash and flames, I silently recited the same prayer that I had prayed all day: If it was my time to die, then I was ready. Up until then I had had an amazing, fulfilling life, for which I was grateful. In welcoming and accepting the thought of my death, I felt no fear at all.

Michael and I walked around for hours with our first aid kits and saline bags, treating firemen with burned, sooty eyes and small open wounds. We climbed over remnants of smashed jewelry stores and unmanned banks, desperately looking for someone trapped but still breathing. It was a pitch-black night: The soot lay like a blanket across the sky and the power had gone out. We felt like the only people left on earth.

In the late evening hours, we came upon the American Express building, which had been converted into a small disaster-response staging area and morgue. The ground was soaked in mud and water, which oozed over my flip-flops, through my socks, and around my toes as I stumbled to help a fireman. His eyes were bloodshot and full of soot; he looked like the walking dead. He had been working in the Marriott hotel and was the last one to run out before the south tower had come crashing down on top of it. All of his friends were dead. He sat on the ground in despair, a broken man. I whispered words of comfort and stroked his hair as I cleaned his eyes.

The wind created ashy tornadoes that danced around us as we tried to wash the soot out, making our task even more challenging. On top of that, I realized that although my eyes were fully open I couldn't see anything—my eyes were filled with dirt, too. So Michael and I sat face-to-face on a pile of rubble to blindly clean the muck from each other's eyes.

"Darling," I said, "you take me to all the best places."

"Only the best for you, my dear," Michael replied.

As soon as our eyes were fresh, we ventured back into the action.

At 11 p.m. on the evening of September 11, 2001, Michael and I arrived at Firehouse 10. Miraculously, it had been left standing, even though it sat directly across the road from the World Trade Center's southeast corner. Someone's splattered head lay in the rubble just two feet from the main door. Inside, everything was covered in ash, and exhausted firemen lay on the ground, overcome with grief. Firehouse 10 had become their de facto resting place.

Michael and I decided to set up a mini triage station there. We rigged flashlights above our heads with ropes tied to the ceiling and sat on the floor with our bags of saline. Every few hours I would look up to see another fifty weary firefighters wandering in to have us wash out their eyes. They spoke of friends who had died and of how much they loved their wives. One fireman ranted about having lost his fire hat, though it was clear to me that it was not really his hat he was upset about losing. I kissed their foreheads before sending them back into hell.

Neither electricity nor cellphones functioned, so there was no way for any of us to contact our loved ones. This was a huge source of anxiety for many of the firemen, who desperately wanted to get in touch with their families but couldn't bear to leave the disaster area. Fortunately, earlier in the day when I was waiting at City Hall, I had managed to get calls out to my parents in Australia and to close friends, telling them that I was okay and not to worry. Many days later, when I finally returned home, my answering machine was filled with messages from other friends, including a few ex-boyfriends, wondering if I had survived.

The next morning around dawn, Michael and I moved our triage station out of Firehouse 10, which was simply too chaotic and crowded, and set it up in a broken bar called St. Charlie's, located only a block away on Liberty Street. We needed a base to work out of and protect us from the elements, and the bar was the perfect size and location. With a little shove on the front door, we got inside. We cleared a space on the ground and set up our few possessions. Then we found a can of spray paint and made a sign to put outside the front door. It read GROUND ZERO FIRST AID STATION. Eventually, our little hangout became home to any Ground Zero workers who stumbled across it.

Just about every shop window had been smashed by the collapse of the Twin Towers. There were destroyed storefronts with jewelry, cash, and expensive clothing lying everywhere. All any of us wanted, though, were basic necessities such as bottled water and toothbrushes, which we'd grab whenever we could find them. The only store that had remained locked shut was the athletic shoe store on the second floor of the World Financial Center. So, in a strange twist of fate, the one thing I most desperately needed—a solid pair of running shoes—was the one thing I

With Michael Voudoras at our Ground Zero first aid station

couldn't get. By the evening of September 12, my waterlogged feet were in dire need of protection. When two firemen walked by with a dead body on a stretcher, we blessed the body and then took off his size fourteen shoes. I needed them more than he did now. My feet were only a size seven, so Michael cut off the front part for me and my toes wiggled through like creatures poking their heads out of a cave.

We ran purely on adrenaline as the hours raced by and our fatigue increased. It was tough work, but I couldn't bring myself to walk away. I could never have lived with myself if I had. This was a front-line war zone, and every second that passed could mean life or death for someone buried beneath the rubble. Even a million rescue workers wouldn't have been enough to help. Some volunteers left to get supplies or meet loved ones, but they always came back. Most refused to leave until they collapsed in exhaustion and had to be carried out on stretchers.

On the second night, Michael and I and the others who had

joined our camp sat around St. Charlie's broken bar and held hands as we sang patriotic songs by candlelight. We then quietly passed around a bottle of Scotch from behind the bar. For about an hour, I caught some flashes of dreamless sleep against the wall. I woke up with a red rose in my hand. I am still not sure who put it there.

On the morning of September 13, we could still hear people buried alive under the rubble making tapping noises, and this kept us going. Tragically, we had no way to get down to them. Ironworkers dug for hours but made only a small dent in the seemingly bottomless pile of steel.

Many of the friends I had worked with during my days as an investment banker had been in the World Trade Center buildings when the planes hit. Initially, finding them had been my primary motivation for going down to Ground Zero. I quickly discovered that that was the case for many of the volunteers I met. But after only a short time, we each realized that it didn't matter if we knew the victims or not; we wanted to help everyone. "Nobody goes home until we all go home" became our quiet motto. Even after the tapping noises stopped, we never gave up hope.

Michael and I stuck side by side, continuing our work as first aid volunteers. The fires underneath Ground Zero were still burning out of control and black soot filled the air. It smelled ghastly, a combination of dead bodies and burning electrical wire.

By the third day, we had collected a team of ten or so nurses and medics and volunteers who had also somehow snuck across our path. Our gang climbed onto the piles of rubble when the rescue dogs found a body and helped pass small buckets full of rubble and body parts down the long line of hands, sometimes forty workers strong. They led to a dump truck that whisked the remains away to an unknown destination. These lines became known as the "bucket brigades."

Along with a constant stream of firemen and policemen, people from other agencies began to pour into Ground Zero: the FBI, the U.S. Army, the Marines, ironworkers, Con Edison technicians, and medics, just to name a few. Although I was already deeply entrenched in the recovery effort, I now had to contend with the Army, the National Guard, the FBI, the NYPD, the CIA, and a line of large tanks that were locking down Ground Zero and preventing volunteers from entering the destroyed area. At every opening, guards stood with machine guns controlling the flow of people and denying most of them entry, except for certified personnel.

I was just an everyday civilian with no formal credentials other than the will to help. When I heard about the lockdown, it occurred to me that if I left Ground Zero now, I might never make it back in. But after three full days down there, I decided to venture out anyway. I made a stop at a friend's house, where I refueled myself with food and stocked up on supplies.

When I returned, I marched straight past two National Guards with submachine guns, trying hard to look like I belonged there. I knew the work I was doing was probably the most important thing I would ever do in my life, and I was determined to get back to it. Luckily, they didn't stop me.

———

The miserable rains started late on the night of September 13. It was freezing. Everyone had to come off "the pile," as it was too hazardous to work—large chunks of iron debris were still slipping off the surrounding buildings.

I was stuck inside St. Charlie's bar cuddling with a large older nurse under green garbage bags that we hoped would help fight the wind blasting through the broken windows. We lay across three steel chairs and held each other tightly. A few hours later, I woke up and apologized for holding on to her stomach. She replied, "Actually, those were my breasts!" We laughed, regaining our sanity. Then we looked around to find that we had been sleeping in a corner filled with human feces.

The next day, while working on the rubble pile, I heard the voice of an angel calling out in the haze, asking if anyone wanted Kentucky Fried Chicken. I hadn't eaten since having a snack at my friend's house the day before, so I stood up and screamed, "OVER HERE!" I couldn't believe my good fortune: Kentucky Fried Chicken is like crack to me. I sat in the midst of the burned plastic and ash, tearing at my precious piece of meat, its succulent juices running down my filthy face.

Throughout my life, my true friends have always known to bring me a bucket of KFC to make me happy. Jonathon Connors, my good buddy who worked on the 104th floor of the World Trade Center, was one of those friends. As I devoured my piece of chicken, my mind floated to him, and I hoped that he had made it out alive. I picked up my phone. Miraculously, it was one of those rare occasions when I could get a cellphone signal. I made a call to a mutual friend, and learned that there had still been no word to anyone from Jonathon. I knew at that moment that I had lost him. It made me more determined than ever to keep working. I found some sunflowers in a wrecked kosher goods store and asked a Con Edison worker to tie them onto lampposts in remembrance of the dead.

After my minifeast, I found a toothbrush and water in a burned-out store and brushed my teeth while sitting cross-legged in the gutter. When I was done, I tied the toothbrush to my waist with a piece of rope, knowing I'd lose it otherwise. Then I started laughing at myself, imagining how absurd I must have looked. I thought about all the *M*A*S*H* episodes I had watched on TV growing up and how, ironically, they had prepared me for this very moment. I'd learned from them that humor was an important part of surviving a tragedy.

Later that day, policemen manned the nearby Burger King and cooked free burgers for everyone. Weeks later, five-star restaurants like Daniel and the Tribeca Grill started sending down filet mignon meals to the aid workers. New York and the world were unselfishly donating their time, skills, and money to help. I remember someone spoon-feeding me crème brûlée, which sent me to nirvana. Moments like those made me proud to be a New Yorker.

On the fourth day after we'd set up shop in St. Charlie's bar, FEMA came by our little first aid station three times to try to shut us down. They said it was time for "the professional disaster people" to take over and asked all volunteers to leave. We prepared to protest. But then they covered their badges and told us to please stay and do what we could, saying, "We need as much help as we can get." They realized that we were giving the firemen and ironworkers the touch of love—the key ingredient missing from the disaster response manuals.

That afternoon, the firemen brought in an ironworker who had temporarily lost his mind. He had been digging for four days straight without sleep and was overcome with demonic emotions. A psychologist from the FBI tried to speak with him, and then many other doctors and priests tried to calm him down, but without any success.

A nurse and I laid him down. We started smoothing his hair as we held his hands. We listened to him rant until he fell into a gentle sleep. We sat next to him for a few hours, watching over him. When he woke up, it was as if nothing had ever happened. He went quietly back to work on the pile. Like everyone else, he didn't want to leave; the job wasn't finished yet.

There were bankers, waiters, lawyers, animators, actors, mums, ad execs, plumbers, singers, and students—people from all walks of life working together. No job was beneath us.

During the first few days, a successful lawyer took charge of cleaning the only functional restroom facilities that I knew of at Ground Zero, located in the makeshift morgue at the American Express building. The bathroom consisted of just six toilets, but was visited regularly by hundreds of workers. He kept it working manually by carrying buckets of water back and forth from the Hudson River. He burned scented candles around the floor so people could see their way in to pee at night. He was there twenty-four hours a day, and he was a true hero. There were many others like him.

One night, I found an old lady pushing a tea trolley around the broken streets. I inquired as to how she had made her way into

Ground Zero. She said that as soon as she had seen the incident on television, she had packed up her car with tea and driven from Chicago. She had told the perimeter guard, "Step aside, sonny," and he had done exactly that. She was eighty-eight years old and she knew that she was needed.

A quiet teenager ran around with sweat dripping from his face, delivering large bottles of water to everyone. His sister had been an illegal immigrant working as a cleaning lady in the restaurant on the top floor of the World Trade Center when the planes hit. He said helping took his mind off her.

The rescue dogs lived in the room next to St. Charlie's bar. Their owners lowered them down into the holes of "the pile" each day to sniff for survivors. They would come back with burned feet and singed tongues, but they, too, always put forth a herculean effort.

It was moments like those, witnessing the actions of the everyday folks on the ground, that melted my soul. They showed that humanity was alive with goodness and that we weren't going to let the terrorists win.

By September 15, we were exhausted and had nothing left to give. But we still had one more thing left to do. All week we had heard rumors of firefighters' body parts yet to be retrieved from the top floors of the Sheraton hotel located across the road from the World Trade Center. So Michael and I and a few other adventurers decided to climb the stairs up to the roof to take care of the issue. Fifty-five haunted floors later, we collapsed, out of breath, wondering how the firemen had done this while loaded down with hundreds of pounds of equipment and breathing smoke.

Stepping to the edge of the roof, we leaned over the railing and

The gates of hell at Ground Zero

found ourselves gazing down into the under-gloom of the gates of hell. I saw a great black pit, as though Satan had risen up out of the earth and scorched everything in his path. Fire and steam came spewing forth from the nostrils of crushed steel, which had the greenish color of bile. Everything was imprisoned in a metal dungeon. I closed my eyes and listened to the cries of a thousand innocent voices. I thought of a quote from Dante's *Inferno: Lasciate ogne speranza voi ch'intrate:* "Abandon all hope, ye who enter here."

The final shutdown of our first aid station came on the afternoon of September 15, when FEMA declared the area unsafe and we were too exhausted to put up a fight. It was time to head home. I walked in a daze from the south facade of the World Trade Center past Century 21, a store about one hundred feet to the east of Ground Zero that had also been badly damaged during the attacks.

As we trudged along, Michael told me that he would catch up with me in a minute; he wanted to go back and get his oxygen tank, which he'd forgotten at St. Charlie's. It never occurred to me that this was good-bye, but once he'd disappeared into the crowds and rubble, we lost track of each other. We didn't see each other again until one year later, at the Ground Zero memorial ceremony.

I was still inside the Ground Zero perimeter when a random stranger offered me a piece of chicken. I thought that was a really nice thing for someone in the street to do. As I sat on the curb eating my chicken, the world fell silent. I was absolutely brain-dead and felt no emotions at all. It was as if I had been in a long dream, and while I'd been trying to wake up, something kept dragging me back in. All around me, fresh workers with shocked faces and clean uniforms were streaming into the Ground Zero area. They stared at my sooty clothes and hair and the tooth-brush, scissors, and selection of first aid tools tied to my waist, and the oxygen tank slung over my back, and they tilted their heads in respect for what I must have been through.

I found my Rollerblades against the Stuyvesant School wall where I had left them five days earlier and started to Rollerblade up the West Side Highway toward my apartment on the Upper East Side. The streets were filled with thousands of New Yorkers who had lined up to show their appreciation for the workers as they left Ground Zero. They held up THANK YOU signs and red, white, and blue streamers and cheered. For the first time since I had entered Ground Zero, I burst out crying in uncontrollable tears. Embarrassed at myself, I skated home as quickly as possible, tears flooding my face, taking darker streets to hide from the light.

CHAPTER 2

I grew up in Australia. My father was an Anglican preacher and a businessman, and my mother was a nurse. They were always flying off to developing countries across the Asia-Pacific region, from the Philippines to Indonesia to Fiji, teaching about God and helping the poor. I was the youngest child of four, so my parents often took me with them on their trips to the jungle while my two brothers, Geoffrey and Stephen, who were only a few years older than me, and my elder sister, Lyndall, stayed behind in school or at work or with relatives.

On those overseas adventures, I shared my showers with frogs and great big water bugs that had eyes the size of quarters and looked like they were going to eat me alive. I ate strange foods, played with kids who didn't speak English, and suffered through many 103-degree fevers.

When I wasn't traveling, I still had an adventuresome childhood. My family lived in a big white house at the edge of the Australian bush. Our extensive gardens led down to a deep river, and across its banks lay one of the largest national parks in the country. My parents had bought the land for next to nothing back when nobody wanted to live out in the middle of nowhere, but soon it flourished into a beautiful estate.

There in the hot, dry Australian bush, our home was threatened by bushfires annually. When the fires started, kangaroos would swim over and come bouncing up into our backyard. My siblings, the neighborhood kids, and I would jump in our tin boats and try to put out the smaller fires on the other side of the river with wet sacks before the flames flew across to our houses.

Throughout my childhood, my strict, religious parents monitored the minds of us four kids but let our bodies run free. On the weekends, Geoffrey, Stephen, and I would canoe across the river into the bush that was our backyard. There, we would camp, climb trees, and swim in secret underground freshwater pools full of turtles and eels. My brothers would jump into the river and chase small sharks with large knives. They played with poisonous snakes and crushed hard-shelled eggs in their mouths. The rest of the time, we played soccer and cricket and every other sport imaginable. We never wore shoes.

My brothers teased me daily. They would pin me down and dribble saliva from their mouths, then suck it back in at the very last second, just before it was about to drop onto my face. Geoffrey and Stephen solved all their problems through humor, and I adored them for it.

When I was ten years old, my brother Stephen talked me into doubling up with him on his bike. We came to a humongous, steep hill and he raced down it at full speed, with me screaming behind him on the seat. I was yelling my head off for him to stop so that I could get off. He just laughed and went faster, which infuriated me. I told him that if he didn't stop, I would jump off the bike. He thought I wouldn't do it, and continued to charge downhill at full throttle. So I jumped off the bike and rolled down the tar road, scraping off layers of my skin along the way. There was a lot of blood, but I had showed him how serious (and stupid!) I really was.

Once, my brothers formed a *Raiders of the Lost Ark* Adventure Club. To become a member, you had to watch the movie twenty-three times, swallow spiders, and jump off forty-foot waterfalls, just like Indiana Jones. I tried several times to join the club, but whenever I met the requirements, they added new ones.

I was an athletic kid, but when it came to adventure, I never could bring myself to take quite the outrageous chances that my brothers took. I had silly fears that always got in the way. I'd jump into bed at night as quickly as possible before the boogie monster living under it could grab me. I'd tuck my hair into my pajamas so that a pair of invisible hands with scissors couldn't reach up to snip off my ponytails.

Geoffrey and Stephen were good-looking guys, and as we grew older, the girls went crazy for them. They had that sort of James Bond confidence that could conquer the world. As teenagers, they went on camping and hitchhiking adventures all over Australia. I admired everything about them.

My brothers also were highly competitive and intelligent, and enjoyed using polysyllabic words to outsmart each other. When they couldn't think of any more impressive words, they would make them up. This kept us all in hysterics at dinnertime, the laughter accompanied by kicks under the dining room table.

My sister, Lyndall, had a very different approach to life from the rest of us kids. She was ten years older than me and loved Alice Cooper and had boyfriends with Harley-Davidsons. She was a naughty preacher's daughter and had a wild, passionate excitement for life. In her younger years, she rejected my parents' doctrine. Even though I didn't always agree with her views, I admired her for her bravery and independence. My parents were irate when she got into trouble with the law for growing large amounts of marijuana.

My father was an immensely talented preacher who would cast quiet spells on his congregation. He would preach in a simple, childlike way, telling exciting stories of the great battles of David and Goliath and of Daniel in the lion's den. He raised his voice during the scary parts and spoke so gently during the suspenseful moments that everyone would have to lean forward in their chairs, eager to hear what was coming next. He would then shout out loud again, and people would almost fall out of their seats. I think he would have made a great actor. In some ways, he already was one.

My father was an honest man who never drank or gambled. He didn't allow us to buy raffle tickets or play soccer on Sundays, but he had the greatest sense of humor and was a terrific athlete. We always won the three-legged race at church picnics.

Yet while everyone adored him and crowded around him after church, I was always a little scared of him. He was a strict, God-fearing man with high blood pressure and a quick temper. His ancestors were sailors and clergymen from Ireland who had been among the first white men to set foot on Australian soil with Governor Phillip, on a ship called *The Sirius*.

My mother was a kind, compassionate woman. She embodied unconditional love and cared more for others than for herself. She never pampered herself, preferring to spend her money and time helping people. She ran a busy geriatric hospital, but despite her packed schedule, she always managed to be there for us. She would cook and clean for all four kids, shuttling us to every sporting event and activity, and also find time to toil in our huge garden creating the most beautiful flower beds. My father was always traveling or working, but despite his frequent absences—or perhaps thanks to them—my parents remained totally in love.

My mother and I had a special bond all my life. She would take me on bush walks, naming the different varieties of flowers and wildlife. She would lead me to our favorite waterfall, talking about poetry and music. She spoke of the beautiful, positive things in life and sheltered me from the bad. She fervently believed that good would overcome evil, as my father preached.

Growing up, I was never allowed to watch scary movies. If a TV show had a swear word in it, my mother would change the channel. I remember the first time I swore, when I was about fourteen. My mother sent me to my room for hours and gave me the Bible to read. The irony, of course, was that the Bible was full of terrifying stories: demons riding on three-headed horses, villains being thrown into burning sulfur lakes, prostitutes, and cities turning into salt—all the things in the world that my parents were attempting to shelter me from. My imagination exploded with images far more graphic than any movie ever could have designed. I often woke up from my dreams exhausted from the previous night's adventures.

Throughout my childhood, my mother's hospital was my playground. When we weren't traveling overseas, I spent hundreds of hours there, including most of my holidays. There were around one hundred senior citizens living in the facility. While most little girls played with dolls, my playmates were these patients. I would walk around the wards and visit everyone, talking with them while they handed me candy. After I'd stopped by forty or so rooms, my pockets would be overloaded. I truly loved the old people. They treated me like their granddaughter. I would secretly tell them all that they were my favorite, and would lay my head in their laps and let them stroke my hair. I would dance for them and paint their nails and brush their hair.

Many of the old people were neglected and alone. Half of them had Alzheimer's and dementia. Each time I visited those patients, it was like they were meeting me for the first time; they were surprised when I guessed so much about their lives, as if by magic. A kind blind lady knew me by the sound of my footsteps. I would try really hard to mix up my stride when I walked past her room, but she always knew I was the one sneaking in to see her.

When I was sixteen, I started officially working part-time at the hospital as a nurse's aide. I was proud of my beautiful nurse's uniform, which was a knee-length pale pink dress. I walked the hospital halls carrying bedpans as if they were laden with treasures.

Not long after I began, I saw a dead body for the first time. I walked into a room where the nurses were filling up open orifices on a fresh corpse, which they did so that fluids wouldn't leak out. I was fascinated by the color of the dead woman's skin and how her eyes were still wide open. When the nurses rolled her over, a great sound escaped her lungs. "She's alive, she's alive!" I cried, as the nurses shuffled me off down the hall and closed the door.

My parents tried very hard to shelter me and my siblings from the bad in the world. Later I learned that living in a bubble isn't necessarily a good thing. Eventually, any bubble is bound to burst. Mine burst a few years after I had graduated from teacher's college at age twenty-two. I was a passenger in a small bus, returning with my cricket team from the state championships, which we had just won. The driver was our coach, who had been drinking all day. Suddenly, he lost control of the wheel and crashed into a retaining wall, causing the van to flip and roll over. There were no seat belts on those kinds of vehicles at the time, so I went flying and felt my legs smash against the steel seats in front of me. Then I hit my head and blacked out.

When I came to, I saw smoke filling the bus. I pushed at the large side windows and got several open for me and my team-mates to crawl out of. I walked in a daze down the highway until my legs gave way and I collapsed on the median strip. A news crew arrived on the scene and asked me questions until the ambulances came and pushed them away.

Over the following days, doctors revealed that the nerves in my legs from the knees down were badly damaged. Time would tell if and how well they would heal. In the meantime, I had lost the use of my legs and was confined to bed.

I had married my college sweetheart only a few weeks prior to the accident. Now I was totally reliant on him for everything. Even the smallest activity had become a monumental chore, requiring a great deal of skill and planning. Tragically, my new husband snapped under the pressure of caring for an invalid. He often left me alone for most of the day and night while he worked, went out drinking with his mates, or played sports. I had to fend for myself. Once, I lay for half a day soaking in menstrual blood because I couldn't get to the toilet. Before I received a wheelchair, I learned to crawl out of bed and onto the floor. Then I'd move on my stomach like a snake, contorting my body up onto the toilet, where I would sit for hours until I had enough energy to pull myself back into bed.

Every morning, I woke up to a world filled with pain and suffering. I couldn't reach most of the food, which was placed high up in the kitchen cupboards, so I often would sit hungry on the floor, crying. On an already slim frame, I lost forty pounds—and I nearly lost my mind. I was in agony and I wanted to die. Self-pity and anger at my new husband slithered in. I was heartbroken that he couldn't look after me. After several months, he left me. Things like this weren't supposed to happen in my beautiful world.

For weeks, I sobbed against the large window in my bedroom, where dribble and dried tears fogged my view. I strained to see out the window, looking for some sign of my husband's return. Hours later, I would give up and slump back into my bed of self-pity.

I needed a lot of care, so I soon moved back in with my parents. They were nonjudgmental and cared for me deeply, but I still carried a deep sense of embarrassment at the failure of my marriage. The hardest part about living back at home was watching my brothers interact with their new wives, kissing each other and looking so much in love. It would remind me of my broken heart, and I would have to leave the dinner table. I continued to cry every day for the next six months, and had permanent marks on my face from where the tears ran down my cheeks. I was inconsolable. The pain in my heart felt physical, like a knife was actually stuck in my chest, ripping at my insides.

Then one day I suddenly stopped crying. I felt an overwhelming sense of peace. I realized that I had lost the life I loved but that the accident hadn't taken my soul. I believe in a divine creator, and I know that God pulled my soul through to a place where things became more bearable. I felt a warm sense of not being alone. A light came on inside me, and I decided to live and to heal.

I went back to teaching math at the local high school, where I had worked before the accident. The school set me up in a classroom on the ground floor, where I could easily maneuver my wheelchair, and the students would push me around and carry my books. Slowly, my heart healed and I regained the use of my legs, until at last I could walk normally. I felt alive again.

I often have thought about the darkness of those years and what the experience brought me. I have realized that from that time forward, I couldn't imagine facing anything worse than what I had already been through. Although I had suffered greatly, I hadn't turned to drugs or alcohol. I had found a way to survive, and had connected to a deep, unshakable faith in myself and in God. And things had gotten better. I had no reason to fear for my life or whatever might come my way.

What I did do, once I recovered, was make up my mind to change continents. My parents were good people, but I longed to move forward into the world outside my childhood bubble. I was now in my mid-twenties; it was time to grow up.

I resolved to make a fresh start in America. Starting over would bring a whole new set of challenges, but at least I would know that I was on my own and that I could learn from my mistakes. I limped out of my old life and into one of my own creation.

CHAPTER 3

When I woke up from my dead sleep two days after returning home from Ground Zero, I felt a deep sense of guilt for being alive. I was in my mid-thirties and my life had already been a full one. I would have willingly swapped it to save anyone in those buildings. The guilt consumed me. I screened my phone calls, talking only to my family and a few friends. I didn't leave my apartment for a week. I felt that if I shut out New York, I would be able to shut out all the hurt that hung in the air like bad meat on a sweltering day. I turned on the television and watched the tragedy for the first time through someone else's eyes. I cried until no more tears came out.

On the seventh day, I was ready to talk. My New York friends had heard about my adventures through my friend Katie and wanted to know if I was okay. They decided to cheer me up by giving me tickets to *The Daily Show with Jon Stewart*. Waiting in the show's lobby, I met a woman named Samantha Aezen. She was working for the American Red Cross New York chapter and had some cards that children had written to the Ground Zero workers. She handed me one from a little girl that said: "If you have a broken heart, you can have mine."

After a short conversation with Samantha, I decided to join up with the American Red Cross the next day and head back to Ground Zero. I had felt a strange impulse all week to go back to help, and I realized that the Red Cross might be the only way I could gain official access.

I placed my plans for my just-completed feature film on hold in order to volunteer. After all, my primary film investor and dear friend Jonathon Connors had now been declared dead. Every little detail in my life seemed shallow and insignificant compared to the important work I could be doing at Ground Zero.

I also had broken up with my boyfriend seven months earlier and had no one to come home to anyway. Nearly all of the volunteers who worked at Ground Zero had children and partners, but they felt called to a higher cause, and their families respected their decision. With my relative freedom, both in terms of home and work life, I felt that I had absolutely no excuse not to pour my heart into the recovery efforts.

I had about $10,000 in the bank. I knew that would be enough to cover several months of rent and expenses, and I felt confident that I would be able to stretch the funds somehow. Many of the volunteers, including myself, later found themselves short on cash, but relatives and friends came through to help us out.

The American Red Cross based their volunteer operations out of their Brooklyn chapter, just across the Brooklyn Bridge from Manhattan. All you needed to join was proof that you were over twenty-one years old and a bill stating that you were currently living in New York. They were so busy that, as far as I could tell, they were allowing every type of person in New York into their organization.

I mentioned my time at Ground Zero and expressed interest in returning to the innermost zone. They took my photo and made me sign a few documents promising to conduct myself in an appropriate manner. Then they signed me up to be a basic volunteer, with the understanding that I could be doing anything from feeding people to making coffee to loading trucks. It didn't matter what chore they gave me, I just wanted to help in any way that I could. Happily, I got a full access Ground Zero badge with a green bar across it. The others, which had a yellow bar across them, meant that you were not allowed into restricted areas of Ground Zero.

I wore my green bar badge with pride as I lined up outside the Brooklyn Red Cross building with sixty other volunteers waiting to be bused back into Ground Zero. As we were driving over the Brooklyn Bridge, a hush fell over us. There was the familiar Manhattan skyline, only the famous World Trade Center landmarks were gone.

When the buses pulled up at the entrance to the restricted zone, we could see that another city had developed within the city of New York. It was to become my home for the next nine months. I worked down there seven days a week, sometimes eighteen hours a day. At night, a bus would drive me and the other volunteers back uptown, dropping us off near the areas where we lived. I would collapse into my bed, often still in my work clothes, for four or five hours of oblivion. Then I would mechanically get up, shower, and do it all over again the next day.

In the mornings, I would take the long subway ride from the Upper East Side to the Lower West Side of Manhattan. Going from uptown to downtown was a complete culture shock. Uptown, people were slowly and respectfully beginning to go about their business, eating in restaurants and returning to a quiet normalcy. Downtown was still a third-world disaster zone. Ground Zero had become an obsession for all of us volunteers, many of whom shared the common goal of finding loved ones we had lost in the attack. The gigantic mess seemed normal to us, while life uptown seemed bizarre.

I found that for the first time in my eleven years of living in New York, strangers talked to one another on the subway. The events of September 11 consumed everyone's conversations. I carried my construction hat and Red Cross vest and badge, so I was easily identifiable as a volunteer working at Ground Zero. Commuters often would approach me, telling me stories of dead relatives or friends or how they had escaped on that fatal day. One morning on the subway, I felt overwhelmed with sadness and started crying uncontrollably. Three people immediately crowded around me, offering comfort.

On the day of my friend Jonathon Connors's funeral, thirty-six other funerals were also held for September 11 victims in the suburb of Cold Spring Harbor, Long Island, alone. In those first months after the attack, thousands of funerals took place, many without caskets since there weren't enough bodies to go around.

When I arrived at the church for Jonathon's memorial service, I saw him standing right there in front of me, alive and breathing. My heart swelled and tears squirted out as I raced over to hug him. I wondered how it could be true that he had survived after all! But then I quickly discovered what nobody had told me: Jonathon had a twin brother. He had never mentioned it to me before. I spent much of the devastating service sneaking suspicious looks at this living ghost through the mourning crowd.

———

The American Red Cross is a traditional organization. They generally gave women the roles of caregivers, while asking male volunteers to load trucks, stock supplies, and do the more "manly" jobs.

I was based at Respite One in the hot zone of Ground Zero, below the National Guard checkpoint at St. John's University on Warren Street. The female Red Cross volunteers there provided comfort—our job was to smile and keep the workers' spirits high. We looked after all the workers involved in the massive cleanup of Ground Zero. Most of them refused to take breaks even to sleep and eat. We would gently insist on feeding them, clothing them, and getting them to sleep on the stretchers we had prepared. Our station was open twenty-four hours a day. It had a television room with couches, Internet-equipped computers, and phones to call home, since many of the ironworkers had traveled here from hundreds of miles away. It also had shower rooms. We gave out all sorts of supplies, from hard hats to gloves, socks, pants, shirts, and toiletries.

Upstairs, we had sleeping rooms with cots and a poster in the hallway that said QUIET ZONE. The lights were always turned down low. On each cot, we placed a blanket, a pillow, a gift bag of hygiene items, and a thank-you note from a schoolchild. I worked upstairs preparing beds and tucking in tired workers, fussing to move the blankets around them as my mother had done for me as a small child and as I had done as a teenager for the elderly folks in my mother's hospital. When the workers passed out, we slipped their shoes off and changed their socks.

The station had a dining area with free food. Many of the fancy restaurants around town sent free meals to us daily, and other businesses such as Target, Poland Springs, Hershey's, and Coca-Cola stocked our tables with snacks and drinks. I lived on Red Bull, Snickers, Milky Ways, and peanut M&M's, and ended up putting on about ten unwanted pounds.

All the volunteers and workers were part of a big family now. We gave one another that familiar "Ground Zero look." It was a glance exchanged without words that said we were all in this together and somehow we would pull through. We loved one another through our souls and shared daily stories from the battlefield.

One of my favorite workers was a retired firefighter named Paul Giedal who was filled with the hope of finding his son Gary, who had been working at Rescue One on September 11. At the end of the day he would say, "We didn't find him today, Alison, but tomorrow we will." He worked down there every single day, digging for his son. He never did find Gary, but he channeled his grief into helping others.

Every day, the female volunteers would drive a golf cart deep into the Ground Zero pit to serve the workers freshly baked cookies and a pot of hot coffee. One day, I announced to the workers that they could have anything they wanted. An older, hefty ironworker walked over to me, picked me up and threw me over his back, and carried me off, to everyone's howls of laughter. Another day a fireman came in with a twenty-inch dildo and an unbroken bottle of champagne they had found inside the wreckage. We all joked about the sort of party we could throw.

Everyone found great comfort in the letters from children that came flooding in from all over the world. Samantha and I would sort the letters and hang them wherever we could. We tucked them into ironworkers' pockets and under the windshields of their cars. Hard men of steel melted into warm pools of love and tears as they quietly read these precious messages, which said things like, "Dear hero, I know how you feel. My goldfish also died that day," or "I am so proud of you my guts hurt inside."

One little girl wrote:

> My dad was a firefighter and he was in Tower One when it collapsed, so it really means a lot to me what you are doing. If it weren't for all of you, my dad would have had no chance of surviving at all. Even though you didn't find him, I still appreciate what you did for everyone else who needed you too. Thank you for working so hard.

Another little girl wrote:

> You are all precious people and you should smile up at them [the ones who died] once a day to tell them you are okay. Everyone here loves you and if you need me I will come and hold you. I have extra love that I can give you. Do you need it? P.S. Come to Vermont and we will show you the beauty of the world again. I have space in my bedroom.

The children's cards were the morphine of Ground Zero, easing our pain. Then, in late September when the Anthrax scares occurred, special government agents came to the Center to warn us that poisonous powder may have been planted inside the letters. By then, Samantha and I had already opened thousands of envelopes. We stared down at our hands and began to laugh, just a bit at first, then hysterically, until tears came out of our eyes. Here we'd thought we had the safest job at Ground Zero!

I could sense when the workers had recovered a lot of bodies. The air would thicken like concrete. On those days, we'd quietly fuss over the workers even more than usual, making an extra effort to smile and find them special sweets.

On one particularly heavy day, the ironworkers finally made it to the ground floor of one of the towers, which had been pushed eight stories underground. There they found twenty bodies. The scratch marks on the walls clearly showed that the trapped people had tried desperately to dig their way out by hand.

On November 4, 2001, the New York Yankees were up against the Arizona Diamondbacks in the World Series. If there had ever been a year for the Yankees to win the baseball pennant, then this was the one. It was probably the first time in history when fans outside of New York were rooting for the Yankees, hoping that the win would lift the spirits of a city in mourning. Nobody worked on the pile that night. Everyone huddled around the televisions set up at Ground Zero. The series was tied at three games apiece, setting up a seven-inning pitching duel between the Yankees' Roger Clemens and the Diamondbacks' Curt Schilling.

In the ninth inning, the Yankees seemed poised to capture their fourth straight World Series title. But then Arizona tied the game, and at the last pitch, Luis Gonzalez looped Rivera's famous cut fastball just over the head of shortstop Derek Jeter. The ball barely reached the outfield grass, but counted for a single and sent Cummings safely to home plate. The game was over. The Diamondbacks had won the World Series. New York grieved with all the pent-up emotions of the past month. What had once been a room filled with excitement fell silent. Grown men cried. Somehow we'd all thought that this win would symbolize great hope for New York. A dark gloom fell over Ground Zero once more.

Romances sprang up between Ground Zero workers. On the third floor of our Red Cross building, a makeshift "hook-up room" even came into existence—a small, quiet space where couples would go to hang out privately and have sex. Every now and then, I would see a couple emerge from the room, switching the light back on, on their way out. We turned a blind eye because we knew that people needed the release. This was still New York City, after all, and hormones, as usual, were raging in full force.

The last thing on my mind, however, was sex; the experience was just too horrific for me. I couldn't look at anyone in a romantic way. It's true that I was wearing more Chanel No. 5 than usual, but it was only to cover up the smell of death, which filled every membrane of my body. I focused on connecting to others through the unconditional love my mother had always shown to me and to her hospital patients.

When the American Red Cross building shut down its services in the Red Zone in March of 2002, Samantha and I were not ready to stop working, so we simply moved across the road to volunteer in the Salvation Army's 35,000-square-foot tent at West and Vesey Streets. Ground Zero was our home, and it felt healing to be there. We felt like the nurses in an old war movie. Our mission was clear: to stand by our brothers to the end.

And so Samantha and I continued on, handing out children's cards and sitting for long hours with the workers, listening to their pain and crying with them. Each night when I traveled back uptown, I observed that New Yorkers were a gentler people now. The car horns hadn't yet started blasting again. Through my own eyes on this tragedy, I glimpsed an inspiring vision of humanity, one filled with hope.

Around that time, the tribute of lights was created. It had eighty-eight mega-bulbs that formed two commemorative fingers of light resembling the Twin Towers, which beamed seven miles into the sky above Manhattan. One night, I stood right in the middle of the base of those powerful lights and looked up to see a real jet plane flying through them. This time, the towers were invincible.

On May 30, 2002, the night before the closing ceremony at Ground Zero, Samantha and I walked down into the pit one last time to share a quiet moment writing messages on the only remaining steel beam, which would be removed as part of the celebration the following day. All the other debris had already been cleared and the site was ready for rebuilding. A priest and a rabbi prayed near us, and at that very second a white speckled pigeon flew over and sat on top of the beam. It was the first sign of wildlife I had seen at Ground Zero in the nine long months I'd worked there. I had been looking for the signs, yet not even one creepy cockroach had wandered into the area until that night.

The next day was the closing ceremony. I woke up at 5 a.m. to meet the other Salvation Army volunteer women on the corner of Murray Street. We walked over to where an unfamiliar SWAT agent clad in black ninja-like fatigues blocked our entrance to Ground Zero. He held up his M-16 automatic weapon and refused us entry. We tried other entrances, but everywhere we went, the Secret Service shut us out. They explained that it was a

ceremony only for "the heroes of Ground Zero," and so the firemen and policemen were the only ones allowed entry. We tried to
explain that we had also worked down there, but our protests fell
on protocol-stuffed ears.

We walked back up the street, elephant heads slung low, miserable at being shut out from the much-needed closing ritual.
Half a mile up the street, we found some portable toilets and
climbed on top of them for better viewing, but we could only
imagine what was going on at the ceremonies down the road.

When the service was over, we were delighted to see the police
and fire departments marching in full armor up the long street
toward us. We jumped to our feet on top of the port-a-potties and
started cheering wildly as the parade sailed by us. I waved to my
old friend Paul, and he smiled and motioned for the other firefighters to look our way.

It was a magical moment. As if on cue in a Hollywood film,
the entire fire department turned and saluted us with their white
gloves. They gave us that "Ground Zero look" that had bonded us
all together for so long. Then they tossed their hats in the air and
tears flowed from our eyes.

Volunteering at Ground Zero was the first time I had worked
alone on a mission of my own choosing. Throughout my childhood and young adult years, I had participated in projects that
my parents or friends had created. But helping out with the post-
9/11 rebuilding efforts in New York City had been my idea and
my solo effort. It also showed me that everyone—from an old
lady with a tea cart, to a middle-aged lawyer willing to clean toilets, to children with love in their hearts—is needed.

ACT II

THE THIRD WAVE

CHAPTER 4

After having come so close to death during the cricket bus accident in Australia, I found that I was able to push the boundaries in my life. I discovered that I had a powerful ability to move on and not dwell on the past. I became more adventurous. My heart was a lot tougher, and I became determined never to give up at anything.

After leaving Australia, I'd moved to New York and decided to make Manhattan my home. I started my new life with barely anything, so the only direction I had to go was up. New York was a competitive town, with the best of the best from around the world all aiming to be top-notch at what they did, and I loved that energy. I was there for the thrill, and I was moving at a different pace than I ever had before. My intellect was stimulated. I felt happy to be alive.

I found a cheap room to rent from an eighty-eight-year-old man who owned a large apartment on the Upper West Side. He treated me like his granddaughter and reminded me of my childhood friends at my mother's hospital for the elderly. Every morning, I would lead him through a modified exercise class in his living room, instructing him to lift his arms and legs as he sat in a chair. He had no family, so when he was sick, I took him to the doctor and the dentist. It was a wonderful situation.

Then I started noticing signs of early stage Alzheimer's, which I recognized from my nursing days. I ignored them until I arrived home one day to find that the old man had changed the front door locks. I couldn't get into my apartment. The doorman acknowledged to the police that I had been living there, so they allowed me to enter in order to retrieve my clothes and few belongings. But once I got inside, I saw that there were no signs of my ever having existed. All my possessions were gone. The man had forgotten who I was and had thrown everything out.

I was flabbergasted and alone, with nothing and nowhere to go. I'd been in New York only a month and didn't have any real friends I could turn to. I wasn't so bothered about losing my clothes, but the loss of my personal items and family photos made me cry. Also gone were phone numbers I had collected of all the people I had met so far in the United States.

Just like that, I was homeless. I lived on the streets for four days. I walked around at night talking to safe-looking strangers and fell asleep during the day on the chairs outside the ladies' powder room at Bloomingdale's. I had so little money that I would watch people eating to feel full.

On the fourth day, I signed up for a free day membership at the New York Sports Club and went inside to take a shower and read the newspaper. I found and applied for a job as a nanny on Park Avenue, and was hired straightaway. I went to live with a Jewish family with twin ten-year-old boys, and I was back on my feet. I had a roof over my head and some spending money again.

Over the next few years, I tried a variety of jobs, from piano teacher to mathematics assistant to a professor at a college. Eventually I landed a job as an investment banker on Wall Street. It was an entry-level job, working in IPOs for a vice president, but I felt excited to be going there every day. I steadily moved up the corporate ladder to jobs with higher pay and more responsibility. I also received a large third-party insurance settlement from my bus accident, and invested it in land and stock options.

The inclination to be a filmmaker didn't strike me until I was in my early thirties. I bought a video camera and took it with me everywhere I went, interviewing everyone from taxi drivers to bums sitting in the streets. I loved to look through the lens and capture people going about their everyday lives.

Thanks to my banking job, I was making a good salary and leading quite a jet-setting lifestyle, but the job didn't fit my personality. So, when I was in my mid-thirties, I quit my secure job and decided to try to make it at something I was really passionate about. I signed up for an intensive fifteen-week course at NYU film school. I had no background other than the amateur films I had taken with my handheld camera, but I soon discovered that I could draw on all of my skills and life experiences—from teaching, to nursing, to travel, to photography—and combine them into storytelling.

A few months after the course ended, I helped raise one million dollars from my Wall Street banker friends to make my first comedy feature film. Shot in the streets of New York, it was called *High Times Potluck* and was written by *Summer of Sam* author Victor Colicchio. It was a fun, lighthearted movie about a suitcase of marijuana and the mob. I secretly dedicated the film to my sister, Lyndall, who had been busted for growing pot when she was a teenager. I was finishing up filming that project when the September 11 attacks happened.

In New York, I dated different types of men from all over the world. All of my romantic relationships were long-term. They usually ended when the guy had to move interstate or overseas for work, and I wasn't ready to follow, attached as I was to New York. I let a few of my soul mates slip away, but I didn't know it at the time.

In late 2002, I met Oscar. I was showing my film *High Times Potluck* in Toronto, where he was also showing his film. We met in the middle of a large crowd at my film party. He reached over and grabbed my arm, gently pulling me over, and started speaking with his charming Italian accent. Toward the end of the night, we kissed passionately against the wall. He was Sicilian and sexy and a fantastic break-dancer. He danced his way into my life.

Oscar and I were pretty much inseparable after that. He had an unbelievable way with children and animals, but was also always broke, just like most of the guys I had dated. Still, we never seemed to need any money to have fun. Oscar was romantic and a great cook. He would come up with creative ideas about where to picnic around New York. Also, he could fix anything. He found broken bicycles in the street and painted them bright yellow with daisies. We would cycle for hours around the city in the snow, laughing and falling off and getting into stupid situations. He reminded me of my adventurous brothers, with a touch of my quick-tempered father thrown in as well.

CHAPTER 5

Christmas has always been my favorite time of year, and no other city I know celebrates it like New York. The Salvation Army donation bells ring out on every street corner and the smell of chestnuts sizzles up my nose. Elaborate window dressings romance shoppers and winter snow fights break out between strangers in Central Park. There are black-tie parties with friends and horse-drawn-carriage rides through slushy streets.

Christmas 2004 was a slightly bleaker season for me than usual, as Oscar and I were both broke. Oscar was between jobs producing films and had taken up bartending at a local Italian restaurant. Meanwhile, I was a trailing director for the TV drama *Law & Order*. I had to observe the other directors on set to make sure the show was shot in the same manner as it had been for the past twenty years. Unfortunately, I had spent the past twelve weeks on set shooting at Chelsea Piers—with no pay.

But we managed to smile through it. Christmas had become way too overcommercialized anyway, we rationalized, so our nearly depleted savings would bring us back to a simpler holiday.

We decided that this year, we could buy each other only one gift, which had to be purchased for twenty dollars or less. I gave Oscar gumboots and he gave me his favorite soccer jersey from his beloved Palermo team and a box of chocolates. Soccer is a religion for Italians and most would sell their mothers before giving away their favorite soccer jerseys. I wore my new jersey proudly as I cooked a succulent chicken, golden baked potatoes, and vegetables for dinner.

We did splurge on a real Christmas tree, which we decorated with photos of our friends and family. I also hung a few of the precious paper angels that I had saved from the September 11 Christmas tree at Ground Zero. The angel decorations had been made by schoolchildren from all over America and sent to the rescue workers to cheer us up. Our tree was mesmerizing. I sat watching it for hours and filmed it on my video camera. At Christmas I became a little girl again.

I thought of Christmas in Australia, which arrived in the middle of summer. Santa Claus would come on water skis. On Christmas Eve, we would go from door to door singing Christmas carols with friends and visit sick people at local hospitals. We would leave milk and cookies for Santa and wake up the next day to find a stocking full of candy on our beds. We would race downstairs and sit like puppies under the tree ready to rip open the presents, which we had already poked holes in with anticipation. At dinner we ate cold meats, lobster, and salads, and after church we played cricket on the beach.

On Christmas this year, it was snowing outside. I lay around in love beneath the tree while Oscar hand-fed me Italian Baci chocolates. Inside the blue wrappers were romantic messages for lovers translated into four languages.

But my bubble burst on Christmas afternoon when I looked at the news on the Internet and saw that a 9.3-magnitude earthquake had struck the sea near Indonesia, triggering a massive tsunami to hit much of southern Asia. The Internet reported that over a thousand people were dead. As each hour passed, that number grew. Soon it reached 5,000, and it kept climbing. I thought about how that was 2,000 more deaths than on September 11 and what a serious disaster it must be.

Oscar and I sat in a trance as events unraveled before our eyes. The death toll climbed to 10,000 and kept going. We were hypnotized by CNN, watching it twenty-four hours a day. The television reports were uncensored. They showed hundreds of dead bodies lying in the streets and wounded people walking around in a daze. CNN anchor Anderson Cooper was reporting from a pile of rubble when he stopped mid-sentence to acknowledge a bad smell coming from beneath him. He said he thought there was a body under the very spot where he was standing.

It was during Cooper's report that I realized I had to go to Asia to help. I called my mother to tell her about my decision, and she responded by saying that she already knew I would be going. She gave me her blessing.

Later that night, I turned to Oscar and told him I was leaving to help and asked if he would like to come with me. I said it was okay if he didn't want to, but I was going anyway. He thought about it for a few hours and then said yes. I was happy he agreed to come on the adventure, but since he had never done anything like it before, I wondered if volunteering together would put a strain on our relationship.

We began talking about the logistics of getting there and gathering the necessary medical supplies. Money was another problem, but I already knew that if you want something badly enough and summon up all the faith and courage inside of you, the whole universe opens up for you.

The next day, Oscar called his parents. They were upset at the idea of him going to Asia and advised against it. His mother was so worried that she wouldn't send any money to help with the journey, hoping to discourage him. Oscar and I started calling our wealthier friends about the possibility of using their frequent flyer miles to get our plane tickets. I also contacted my health-care worker friends at local hospitals and began collecting basic medical supplies.

We then visited a World Health Organization doctor so that we could get the booster injections we needed. I was nervous about not having the money to pay the doctor's bill, but I kept my faith that somehow I would be able to pay later. When the nurse giving us the injections heard about our plan, she gave us some of the treatments for free, adding in extra ciprofloxacin antibiotics and diarrhea pills.

Next, we had to decide where to go. We chose Sri Lanka because it was an extremely poor, small country and wouldn't receive as much assistance from its own government or international aid organizations as the other countries that had been hit, such as India and Thailand. Some of my friends had been on surfing trips to Sri Lanka, and they had told me shocking stories of the poverty and horrible hospital conditions there. I read that although the coastline had been devastated, there were still places in the capital city of Colombo where one could buy food and supplies, so I found a cheap hotel online where we could stay the first night, and printed out road maps of Sri Lanka from the

Internet. We would head out to the affected areas after we'd had a chance to stock up.

Later that week, my friend Samantha brought us sleeping bags and walkie-talkies. We packed those along with our other basic necessities—a first aid kit, medications, rubber gloves, waterproof matches, and flashlights. We had to be ready to camp out in the wild if necessary. Of course, I also threw in my bottle of Chanel No. 5. I packed my handheld video camera, thinking it would be useful for taking some shots of the tsunami damage. That way, I figured, we could hold a small fund-raiser when we returned to New York a few weeks later. Noticeably missing from my gear were plane tickets and spending money, but those were only minor details. I knew that I was going to make it there somehow.

I continued to watch the disaster day after day on TV. I couldn't believe it when the reporters said that the death toll had now reached over 100,000 people. It made me sick with frustration to think about how every second I sat in my apartment could mean life or death for someone over there.

On New Year's Day, Oscar heard from a friend of a friend in Telluride, Colorado, who knew a chef called Bruce who was also heading over to Sri Lanka. We spoke with Bruce on the phone and coordinated a cooking stove and a few other supplies. We told him to stay in touch about travel plans.

My friend Mark Axelowitz had three children, Nicole, Jared, and Chloe. They had the idea of making hot chocolate to sell outside a grocery store in New York to raise money for the tsunami victims. The next day, the whole family sat outside in zero-degree weather selling hot drinks and cookies. Then Mark and his wife invited me to their home, where his children presented me with $300, half the money they had raised (the rest they were donating to the American Red Cross). I was excited and humbled by his children's actions. It was the only cash donation I received before leaving home.

At 2 a.m. on January 3, 2005, I finally received the phone call I'd been waiting for. It was from my friend Joe in Michigan. He had found me an air ticket and had driven two hours in a snowstorm to the airport to buy it for me. The only hitch, he informed me, was that I had to be at JFK Airport in three hours. I was ready. I turned to Oscar, who still had no clue where his air ticket was coming from, and told him that I needed to leave. I said that he should follow me as soon as he could, and not to give up until he found a ticket.

Two hours later, I set off into the unknown, waving to a nervous Oscar through the rear window of a taxi. I was leaving home with $300 in my pocket, tears leaking out of my eyes, and a heart full of love.

Eighteen hours later, I landed in Singapore to connect with my flight to Sri Lanka, and the airlines informed me that I had a twenty-three-hour layover. It felt like I was finally at the marathon starting line but the race official had yelled, "Ready, set, stop!" Furthermore, Singapore Airlines wasn't going to give me a free room to wait in. I burst into tears like a little girl. I explained my mission to the airline attendee and flashed my September 11 Ground Zero American Red Cross badge, and they quietly slipped me a hotel coupon.

When I got to the hotel, I checked my email. Oscar had written to say that he was now on a flight heading toward me. He had called his friends Tony Detre and Henry Jarecki, who had happened to be at the airport at the time and purchased him a ticket.

Oscar had had two hours to pack and get to the airport. He'd only just made it. The best news was that due to my extended layover, Oscar was able to catch up with me in Singapore. After some long Italian kisses in the airport, we continued on to Colombo together. So far the whole trip had been like watching a magician pull a rabbit, a tiger, and then a jet plane out of an empty hat. The universe unlocked its magic, and we were ready to ride.

Sri Lanka is an island shaped like a large teardrop located to the south of India. The country was called Ceylon under British rule, and its teas are among the finest in the world. It is also a very long way from New York City.

At the baggage claim in Colombo, I met a large, loud man named Donny Paterson. He was an ex–Army engineer and truck driver from Newcastle, Australia, who had come by himself to help the tsunami vicitims. He reminded me of a young Crocodile Dundee. When he told me he was on a mission from God, I saw it as a sign from the universe and asked him to join us. Now the only problem was that I had to go over to my protective Sicilian boyfriend and tell him that I had just invited another man to tag along with us. Surprisingly, Oscar was a good sport about it, so Donny came with us to our pre-booked hotel. He quickly proved a critical addition to our inexperienced team, possessing loads of practical skills, like building and truck driving, that I didn't have.

Bruce French, the chef from Colorado with whom Oscar's friends had connected us, joined us the next day, and we became a team of four volunteers. Bruce was a quiet, muscular outdoorsman in his forties who was shocked to find Donny in his hotel bed when he arrived at 3 a.m. Bruce lived in a yurt in Telluride and was a private chef to Pearl Jam and the Rolling Stones. Cute and well-weathered, Bruce had sailed all over the world and added a calm strength to our gang. He ended up being the voice of reason in our team.

We found the yellow pages, which were actually white, and searched for car rentals. It turned out that there were streets full of rentals close by, so we set off on foot to find a vehicle. After much negotiating and heckling over what in the end was only an extra dollar a day (it sounded like thousands in rupees), we rented a minivan that came with a non-English-speaking Sri Lankan driver. We packed the van with food and water bought from a local supermarket in Colombo and waited anxiously for our driver to meet us at the agreed-upon time of 4 a.m. He arrived two hours late, but at least he made it, and we started driving down the coast to find the tsunami disaster zone. At last, we could get to work.

Australians are loud. I should know: I am one. But Donny was louder than any Australian I had ever known, and he never stopped talking. He had a voice that could be heard in outer space. As he jabbered on for the entire ride down the coast, the rest of us sang along to James Taylor on the van radio as the sun was rising.

It wasn't long until we came upon what used to be the Sri Lankan coastal villages. Everything was gone, like some giant monster had come through and demolished the place. I felt as though I was standing at the gates of hell on September 11 again, only this time there were still people alive whom I could help.

Villagers wandered around looking sad, desperate, and lost. Donny asked if we could stop for a while. We walked around the rubble asking people if they were okay. Donny yelled out, "How are you, machan!" ("Machan" is an old English term that means "my friend.") People cracked a smile as he offered them a cigarette or candy. We didn't have enough water or food for everyone, so Donnie's gifts, a bag of airplane toothbrushes, and big smiles were all we had to give that day. Soon Donny was surrounded by fifty desperate people grabbing at him to get at the goods he was passing out. It was quite a frightening experience and I motioned to the driver to start the van in case we had to make a quick getaway. But the crowd died down when they saw he had nothing left.

Donny and I opened our first aid kits and attended to basic medical needs. It was 105 degrees and Donny was melting over everyone. He bandaged an old man's leg with his cigarette hanging out of his mouth and sweat dripping off his head. Throughout the day, Donny proved to be a caring and competent medic, and I was relieved to have him by my side. Oscar did what he did best: He started performing magic tricks and break-dancing for the children. Bruce listened even though he couldn't understand what people were saying and beamed love all around. He had a gleam in his eye that could soothe anyone.

After hours of hot, sweaty work, we continued driving down the coast in a quiet state of shock. Hundreds of miles of coastline were destroyed and starving people sat around everywhere. Where was the help? Where was the government? Where were the aid groups and the NGOs?

It had been ten days since the tsunami, and we felt very alone.

This was Oscar's first volunteering experience. He had always wanted to do something like this but didn't know how. In those first days, he was excited and nervous. He chain-smoked, not knowing what he was supposed to be doing, but soon felt more at ease performing magic tricks for the children. Donny was retired from the Army and living in the suburbs of Australia with his wife and three teenage kids. He had a restless soul and had a powerful calling to serve others. Bruce had sailed to Sri Lanka years earlier and had made a deep connection with the people, so he had wanted to come back to help them. He made it clear that he didn't want anything to do with first aid—he was there to clear rubble and build. Ever since my experience at Ground Zero, I had been eager to do similar work again. I had learned that when a disaster happens, nobody is really in charge and there are always ways to help.

We stopped at village upon village, and we were surrounded by people with medical needs. A small cut that got infected could lead to amputation and deformity later. There was nowhere for these people to go for treatment; we were their only hope. I was grateful for my nurse's training.

We came to yet another destroyed village called Kosgoda, where people sat around in hopelessness. We cooked rice and handed out water and gave hugs. Donny saved a little turtle that had been trapped in a well and rounded up the village kids to release it back into the sea as a symbol of good luck. On the beach we came across a decaying headless body, which had just washed up out of the ocean. Everybody, including the children, stared in shock. It looked like a boy around ten years old. The corpse had a strange rope tied around its belly, and its feet and hands had been chewed off. And it had an erection. We moved the crowd farther down the beach and released the turtle into the water. It just floated there as if it were dead, so Donny gave it a few hefty pushes and at last it swam out into the ocean. Everybody cheered and the children huddled around us.

Back in the village, a toothless ice-cream man arrived on a rusty bike. He had cycled from somewhere inland. Oscar bought the entire village ice cream, and for a few minutes the world tasted better.

An elderly man from the village walked over to us and introduced himself in English. He told us that long ago, he had traveled to the United States on a ship. He then showed us an old American one-dollar bill covered in plastic, which he kept in his pocket, and offered it to us to help. He had kind eyes but was ashamed about having no teeth, so he covered his mouth with his hand as he spoke. He talked about the tsunami troubles and then introduced us to the village leaders, acting as translator. They told us that it didn't matter if we had nothing to give them; the fact that we had come from the other side of the world from very important countries was enough to give them hope. Then they got on their knees, bowed before us, and started kissing our feet. Later, we found out this was a Sri Lankan custom, but I never did get used to it.

As it started growing dark out, we stopped in a larger town to buy ropes and plastic so that we could rig up a temporary shelter for people to sleep under. In the shop, we met two guys named Luke and Steve, who were pilots from Emirates Airlines. They had been coming to Sri Lanka to surf for years, and when they had heard about the tsunami, they had grabbed their first aid kits and flown over to help. Luke had left his wife and two-month-old baby girl in London. We bonded instantly. They told us about a village they had just found with an overturned train, and mentioned that there was also a town nearby where we could sleep. We all decided to head there right away.

———

The town of Hikkaduwa had been destroyed, but since there was a large reef in front of it to protect it, it wasn't hit as badly as other areas had been. The worst affected villages were the ones where the locals had removed the coral reefs. In those reefless areas, the water surged through and destroyed everything. In Hikkaduwa, on the other hand, many structures were still standing, although the shops and hotels had filled with water and the goods had washed away. Most buildings were boarded up. We found the only guesthouse still open. It was called The Moonbeam and it cost four dollars a night. I felt great about the accommodations, as I had thought we would be spending the night in tents. The news reports had shown only destruction.

There was nowhere to eat, so we opened up our cans of baked beans and pears. We cooked them by flashlight on Bruce's little stove on the pathway outside the guesthouse. It had been a long day. I pulled out my handheld video camera and asked the gang to express their feelings. Our reports reflected the sad situation. Then Oscar asked Donny if he had "had a special moment" that day. Donny said that he hadn't really had time to have a "special moment" that day because he'd been so busy. "But maybe I'll have one later tonight in bed when no one's looking," he said, cracking us all up. Donny's irreverent sense of humor reminded me of my brothers. I knew it would play a large role in getting us through our journey.

We woke up at 5 a.m. to a beautiful sunrise and walked along the beach, staring out into the now tame ocean. Bruce cooked baked beans and eggs we had brought from Colombo. I began to put on my shoes and found a little mouse sleeping in one of them. We then drove back to the village Luke and Steve had told us about, which was located about four miles from the town where we had stayed the night.

The village, which was called Peraliya, had been completely destroyed. A forty-foot tsunami wave had attacked it and overturned a passing train, killing approximately 2,500 people and destroying 510 homes. The wave had also surged up the river and traveled two miles inland. The only remaining structures were the school library and one block of classrooms. As we walked around, villagers who had been sleeping in the open rubble came over to us. They looked like the walking dead. I found a mound of long black hair hanging on a tree. At first I thought it was a wig, but upon closer inspection I discovered it was a real human scalp, just like out of an old American cowboys and Indians movie. The force from the tsunami must have ripped it right off of someone's head.

The overturned train in Peraliya

Nobody spoke English, so we communicated with sign language. The villagers needed clean water, food, shelter, and medical aid. All the wells had been contaminated with salt water, so we began by handing out small rations of bottled water. Children swarmed around me begging for a small plastic lid full of it, and I watched them suck it into their mouths like it was chocolate syrup. My insides twisted as I realized that the situation was far worse than I could have ever imagined. I cried out to God to send every spare angel in heaven and on earth to this hurt area of the world.

Next we started cleaning out the library building, which was completely filled to the roof with broken tables, mangled chairs, and ruined books. Donny found men to help him remove the furniture, while I collected the wet books and laid them out in the sun to dry. Bruce found a ladder and climbed onto the roof to start patching up the huge holes with the tiles he had found on the ground. Steve tried to help him but realized he was scared of heights and came down quickly. The temperature outside was an inferno. Sweat ran down our bodies as we worked.

As the day scorched by, hundreds of people slowly appeared from out of nowhere. They mostly sat around under the trees in shock. I knew from the news reports that many people had lost more than twenty family members to the tsunami. Men had come home from fishing trips to find their entire families and homes washed away. Although I couldn't understand what the villagers were saying, I listened to their stories as I worked, and found that I didn't need to know their language to feel their pain and make them feel heard.

Meanwhile, Oscar surveyed the area. He found a Buddhist temple and walked inside to speak with the monks. Sicilians are generally good at two things: eating and getting stuff. The monks

Donny at our makeshift first aid station

led him to a room with a surprisingly large amount of rice and spices, which Oscar asked for in exchange for medical supplies. I'm not sure if it was a fair trade, but Oscar managed to set up what he called "the restaurant" in a school classroom. Village women helped cook the food in a gigantic pot over an open fire. As soon as it was ready, hundreds of starving villagers inhaled the lunch.

In the afternoon, Luke, Steve, Donny, and I set up a first aid station out of the van by hooking a tent to its side, and we started treating villagers. Soon, dozens of wounded people were lining up for help. One little girl named Nardika had run so fast to get away from the tsunami that she had no skin left on her feet. It took me two hours to clean them, and when I was done, I had a new best friend. From that day on, she rarely left my side.

Just ten hours after we began, we had treated over one hundred people, served a meal, and cleared the library completely. It was a comfort to know that hundreds of people would sleep there tonight. We called it a day and headed back to our guesthouse in the neighboring village. Over another simple dinner of canned food, we held a meeting to discuss what to do next. We all agreed to stay there for at least a few more days instead of driving farther along the coast.

Donny had a plan to build a toilet, which would hopefully reduce the risk of cholera and outbreaks of other diseases. Oscar had been standing in the middle of the highway stopping aid trucks, successfully obtaining food, clothes, and dried milk. So when a bulldozer passed by, he hijacked it, ordering the driver to turn into the village to dig a hole for Donny's toilet.

The toilet was a simply engineered structure consisting of a ten-foot hole in the ground filled with lime, with two planks of wood placed across the top. Donny surrounded it with huge pieces of colored plastic for privacy. In most places in Sri Lanka, there was no toilet paper. It was customary to eat food with your right hand and wipe your bottom with your left hand. If you were seen eating with your left hand, it was considered impolite and unhygienic.

Days crawled by as though they were centuries. We found ourselves running an internally displaced people (IDP) camp caring for over 3,000 people. We were in charge simply because nobody else was. The other volunteers quickly came to learn the lesson I had learned at Ground Zero: If we acted with authority, people would listen. No one ever questioned our authority. What the villagers needed now were leaders, and although we were making it up moment by moment, we kept things moving forward. There were aid organizations working in other far-off places, but this was one of the largest disasters of all time and assistance was spread thin. This was simply way too big of a crisis for the Sri Lankan government and even dozens of NGOs to handle alone.

Dead bodies in all states of decay kept turning up everywhere. In the first week, the locals quickly buried over 3,000 bodies in a shallow grave across the road from the village near the ocean by bulldozing them into a hole on top of one another and then covering it up with a few feet of sand and dirt.

Providing the villagers with food, water, shelter, and medical assistance remained our top priorities. During that first week, we used my friend Mark Axelowitz's children's donation money to buy water and food from stores farther inland that hadn't been destroyed. I felt very grateful for their hard work selling hot chocolate back in New York City.

Luke and Steve soon left us, and it was the four of us alone again. Donny and I moved the first aid station into the library to shelter us from the blistering heat. We turned two bookcases upside down to make them into beds, and I put towels I'd purchased from a village nearby across them to act as sheets. Each day, the hospital lines swelled and I collected a few Dutch doctors whom I had found in the local town to work with us. News of our services quickly spread, and some people walked over twenty miles to see us. Most mornings, we would find thousands of people waiting for us outside the old school library.

I became so busy with the clinic that I barely had time to use the bathroom. Once, I was so absorbed in my work that I accidentally ended up peeing down my legs. There were pregnant women who needed basic healthcare, and babies with danger-ously high temperatures. Some people had broken arms, infec-tions, or respiratory problems. Others had deep cuts and abscesses from glass and other foreign bodies lodged deep inside their skin. I had never sewn up wounds before, but one of the volunteer doctors taught me how.

One of my first patients was a very old man who I had thought was dying. I couldn't work out what was wrong with him. I fussed over him and gave him water and let him sleep in the hos-pital. Hours later, the village chief came in yelling at him and chased him outside. Apparently he was the village drunk and was suffering only from having had too many drinks.

This was a symptom I now recognized and would see over and over again in the coming weeks. The local brew was called *arrack*. It was a strong alcoholic beverage distilled from fermented fruit, grain, sugarcane, or the sap of coconut palms. It tasted like a mixture of whiskey and rum and caused people to hallucinate when drunk in large quantities. In the weeks to come, I saw many volunteers get drunk and aggressive from it.

I ended up developing a deep affection for the village drunks, many of whom had open wounds on their legs just like everyone else did. Sometimes our local staff would try to refuse them entry to the hospital, but when I heard them fighting I would step in and gently guide the drunkards to a corner of the hospital for treatment. One of the drunk men had escaped from the tsunami by climbing up a coconut tree, and now had fifty-three infected wounds on his legs. We called him Godzilla because he always wore a T-shirt with a cartoon of the green monster on it. When Oscar roared playfully at him, he would roar back.

Many people also came in with dog bites, and I wondered if there would be a rabies outbreak. The animals in Peraliya were starving to death. There was hardly any food around for the humans, so the dogs had begun eating the dead bodies. One day I saw a dog running through the village with a human femur in his mouth. I hoped we wouldn't have to start killing the dogs.

There were also injuries that we couldn't see—the emotional ones. There were women who had lost eight children and were suffering immensely. We called our treatment for these people "the tsunami Band-Aid." We would fuss over them, holding their hands and beaming love to them. Children clung to my arms in search of milk and love, but I had only love to offer. I would hide my tears behind my Gucci sunglasses and walk into a broken house to cry where nobody could see me. Then I would walk back wearing a disguise of smiles. Being strong was imperative to the success of the mission. I told myself that I could always go home to New York if it got to be too much.

At the end of the second week, a German disaster relief organization called the Federal Agency for Technical Relief, or THW, arrived in town. Thankfully, they started pumping the wells to clean the water and set up two temporary water tanks, which they tested for E. coli bacteria each day. Now the villagers at least had some limited access to clean water again. Still, we often ran out of water in Peraliya and had to scramble around the coast to find new resources.

The local tap water wasn't filtered and our bodies weren't used to the bacteria found in it, so the volunteers never drank it. We even washed our teeth with bottled water. We never ordered soda or drinks with ice cubes in them, as the ice was made from the unfiltered tap water and people who consumed even such a small amount could become sick very quickly.

Oscar concentrated on obtaining food and water and other goods for the village. As a film producer, he knew how to raise money and put things in order. He was now "producing" a village with the same skills he had used to make his films. One idea he had was to place young boys with donation buckets at the entrance to the village. Each day, rich sightseers from the city would drive down the coast to look at the train wreck and then leave, oblivious to the thousands of starving people standing twenty feet in the other direction. The donation bucket boys worked hard all week and collected 30,000 rupees a day, totaling a precious $300, which we desperately needed to buy the village supplies and tools. Later, while they were counting the money back at the school, Oscar handed them each a dollar for their work. They looked upset by his action, and one by one they all put the money back into the bucket for the village fund. It was a heartwarming moment. Everyone was contributing as best they could. After ten days, the boys stopped seeking donations; the villagers agreed that they didn't want to appear to be beggars.

We were feeding the villagers one meal a day. People lined up for hours in the extreme heat just to get a piece of pumpkin or a cup of rice. It sometimes felt inhumane to me, but then I remembered that at least they were getting something to eat, unlike the thousands of others along the coastline who we couldn't help.

Donny was in charge of removing rubble and clearing the land. He tried to teach his Sri Lankan men the same discipline he had learned in the Australian Army by showing up early for work every morning to beat the sun, but most days the villagers were just too lazy to show up. Donny slaved on with his tasks no matter how many people came to help.

Bruce was a Buddhist and felt it was important to get people back to prayer so that they could take comfort in their faith. Unfortunately, there were hundreds of bodies in the marshes near the Buddhist temple at the back of the village, and the smell of death and decomposition were strong. The foundation of people's spiritual beliefs lay in disarray, filled with over ten feet of mud. Residents had nowhere to pray or mourn departed loved ones, which was crucial to the healing process.

So Bruce spent days laboring with village men to clean out the temple. Women brought them tea while children made games of carrying away the debris. The villagers were nudged out of their shock and lethargy by the energy and support of well-intentioned strangers, including other volunteers who joined in the effort. Bruce had brought Tibetan prayer flags with him, which he hung over the temple once the work was finished, much to the delight of the monks. Traditionally, as you hang prayer flags, you put blessings into them, and when the winds blow through them, they carry your intentions out into the universe. Bruce's intentions were for the people of Sri Lanka to find strength within themselves to carry on, and for the souls of the victims to find their place in light and collective consciousness. I could tell how much the villagers appreciated having their temple back.

Though Peraliya was a Buddhist village, there were some Hindus and Muslims there as well. There was also one Christian woman named Chamilla who turned out to be the only local who spoke English. She became our translator and worked hard in the hospital while her husband looked after her baby.

On our way back to our guesthouse each night or on our trips to the town of Galle, the capital of our region, where we would buy supplies, we would see thousands of people still in need and many places getting no help at all. I always took my first aid kit with me so that I could perform quick services if need be. People would be sitting in the streets with open infected wounds that had flies swarming on them. The flies were everywhere; even the hospital was infested with the dirty little buggers.

Our gang tried for a while to spread out farther along the coast, delivering food, water, and medical supplies to other villages, but we soon became overwhelmed by the size of the job. We realized that we couldn't help everyone; we were only a four-person team, and there were limits to what we could accomplish. We talked about it and agreed that we needed to concentrate just on Peraliya.

I devoted most of my time and energy to the makeshift hospital, where we were seeing over a thousand patients a day. I tied my hair back under a white scarf and drew a red cross on it so that people would know to come to me for first aid. I found a Dutch doctor and two nurses at the Hikkaduwa guesthouse, where a steady stream of volunteers were now arriving, and recruited them to join me. They had acquired several doses of the tetanus vaccine, and I stored the precious serum in a bucket filled with ice that I bought from a town vendor. I carried that blue bucket with me everywhere, making sure the ice didn't melt so the batch wouldn't go bad.

Not long after that, I met two young German doctors, named Sebastian and Henning, at the guesthouse. They were fresh out of medical school and became valuable members of our team. Henning was brilliant at translating the names of the various drugs that were donated by volunteers from all over the world. He built a medicine cabinet and carefully separated and labeled all the drugs. Sebastian created a mobile ambulance out of a tiny three-wheeled vehicle called a tuk-tuk. He placed a German paramedic sticker on the side to make it appear more official, but it still looked like a big toy. Tuk-tuks were the main mode of transportation in the area and were a cheap way to get around. They had no doors, and it could get quite breezy at high speeds. Sebastian and Henning drove off to faraway villages treating people and would sometimes drive them back to the field hospital for further help. Later, Sebastian bought the hospital a refrigerator, which proved to be a major turning point because it allowed us to store important medicines.

As I worked in the hospital, mothers told me heart-wrenching stories of the children who were washed from their arms. I remained strong as my translator stumbled through broken dialogue and women cried into my chest.

I came down with a 103-degree fever for a few days and perspiration flooded my body. Still, I felt there was no time to stop and rest. The villagers had larger problems than mine.

Children surrounded the hospital all day long begging for milk, and when they didn't get my attention, they would pinch my arm or leg really hard until I screamed out in pain and turned to notice them. I had brought paper and pencils with me, which I gave to the children to keep them busy. They started drawing tsunami images with dead bodies and giant waves destroying their homes. I hung the pictures on the hospital walls and the kids drew hundreds more.

Wherever we went, we recruited tourists and expatriates living on the island to come work in our village. In addition, word of our field hospital had spread throughout the region, so people would just show up at our village to offer help. Sometimes volunteers would offer us $100 in cash, but we would give them a list of supplies instead. They would turn around and drive miles inland to find stocked stores, returning by the end of the day like Santa Clauses, bearing bags of the goods we needed. Many journalists who were in the region to report on the situation were so affected by the devastation that they crossed the professional line and started working with us as volunteers or left money for us to buy food.

We soon realized that we had to establish a management system for our relief efforts. On the first day, we had met the village chief and a number of other responsible men. Oscar and Bruce held regular meetings with them through our translator, Chamilla. Together, they formed committees for food distribution and other basic tasks, and chose organizers to be in charge of each one. They drew up long lists of the families in the village to make sure people didn't double up on aid and that everyone was treated fairly. Each day, Oscar and Bruce would hold a meeting with heads of the various committees to discuss camp problems.

Temporary shelters were popping up all over the village, but we were in a race to get people under some sort of roofing before the monsoons came flooding through in March. Bruce serendipitously acquired a large shipment of tents that an NGO had dumped somewhere farther up the coast. Oscar and his committees distributed these to families in the village.

The housing situation improved again when a group from the Danish government called Danish People's Aid came to town and pledged to pay for 700 temporary wooden shelters if we could help provide manpower to build them. Naturally, we said yes. The much-needed temporary shelters were ten feet wide by twelve feet long and often had to house fourteen family members. They were supposed to last only until permanent homes could be arranged. The committees gave temporary housing first to pregnant women and those who had been seriously injured; the rest was based on a lottery system. Even though the shelters had four walls, the villagers still had nothing to put inside. We took a photo of each family to hang on their wall as a new beginning.

In late January, we moved into a new guesthouse that was a dollar a night cheaper, which meant a lot to us at that point. At night we would collapse in excited exhaustion and drink beers and king coconuts around a bonfire on the beach. There were more stars out than could ever be counted.

The town of Hikkaduwa, where our guesthouse was located, was slowly reopening, in large part thanks to the help of the U.S. Marines who were on vacation from the Iraq war. We invited them to Peraliya and asked for satellite photos of the area to see how much damage had been done. The photos revealed that the village was now four feet below sea level, which meant that the area would continually flood. The Marines were in Sri Lanka to restore government facilities and hotels, so unfortunately they didn't have permission to help us clear land. But they did boost our morale and play volleyball with the children in front of the hospital.

Oscar, Donny, Bruce, and I were so overloaded with work that we usually wouldn't even stop to eat during the day. The food in the village was spicy and strange-tasting anyway, and large bugs and other unrecognizable materials would fall into it. So we lived mostly on bananas and the local king coconuts, which were extremely large green and yellow coconuts with clear milk and without the strong coconut taste. Known to cure more than forty-eight diseases, they also made an excellent moisturizer and hair conditioner.

A few mom-and-pop food operations started opening up at the local guesthouses, and they would cook meals for the volunteers. The only problem was that if many hungry volunteers descended on one guesthouse at the same time, it could be hours before we ate. The guesthouse cooks would prepare only one meal at a time and present it to the person before going back inside to cook the next meal. By the time the fourteenth volunteer received his meal, it would be three hours later. I thought it was a very strange way to do things, but we learned to make it work for us by dropping off our dinner orders at least five hours before we planned on eating.

On one particularly busy day at camp, hundreds of children swarmed about the hospital while the adults had their heads deep in worries. Then an Israeli volunteer group came through the village and started playing games with the children designed to release trauma. They were fantastic. The games included a laughter circle where we would all point at one another and laugh, as well as a mime circle where we would pretend to throw gigantic balls at each other. Oscar joined in to play. He would fall on the ground and grunt loudly, leaving the children in hysterics. We linked hands at the end and cried tears of happiness. It was the first time we had heard the children laughing and singing.

That night, we invited the Israeli volunteers to stay at our guesthouse. Some very fine red wines surfaced from their luggage. The Israelis knew firsthand about trauma and what people needed after a long day in the field. We invited them to stay with us longer.

On one particularly hot day, we decided to take the children out of the village and across the road to the ocean for a swim for the first time since the tsunami. We wondered if the children would ever trust the sea again. Oscar led the way, putting on his snorkel and flippers and blowing his whistle. Hundreds of children, parents, volunteers, cats, dogs, and drunks excitedly followed. We crossed the highway and stood on a small piece of soil above the beach. The Israeli volunteers gave the children a large piece of rope with colored flags on it, and they held hands and began to sing and dance in a circle. After that, we headed onto the rocks and climbed down to the sand. I looked back to where we had been singing and realized we'd been on top of the unmarked graves of the 3,000 local tsunami victims. Nobody seemed to have noticed or minded that we had literally been dancing on people's graves. I liked the idea that a joyful ceremony had spontaneously erupted at that very spot.

When we got to the seashore, many of the children began to cry out in fear. They shouted, "Big wave, big wave!" We reassured them that they were safe. We held hands, forming a long line that stretched across the beach, and slowly walked toward the ocean,

Taking the kids to the ocean for the first time after the tsunami

where we began by dipping our toes in the water. There were excited shrieks and many children ran back to the safety of the rock wall. Oscar, Sebastian, and the Israeli volunteers did crazy somersaults into the water, trying to entice the children back into the sea. About thirty boys ended up swimming with them, while most of the girls and very young children stayed at the water's edge, clinging on to me for dear life.

We stayed at the beach for a few hours, the parents watching their brave children from the road. Our first official swimming day was a success, and we followed it with many more.

The chief of the village was a sturdy fisherman with a fleet of boats. Although he was sixty-eight, which is quite old by Sri Lankan standards, he was built like a bronzed god. He had two wives who loved him very much. Years earlier, when the new government had come to power, the secret police had captured him, beat him up, and pulled off his toenails and fingernails. They poured chili powder over him and left him to die in a closed sack. After this, he supposedly escaped and lived for a year in a fishing boat at sea, and then later slept in a secret coffin buried underground. Whether or not the story was true, it was part of the legend that made the chief a beloved leader.

During the tsunami, the chief had lost everything he owned except for one boat, but he always seemed to have plenty of marijuana on him, which made him very popular with some of the volunteers. He would often invite the volunteers over for a fish dinner, and we would sit in his dirty shed and laugh the night away.

We wanted the chief and his leadership committee to feel like an important part of the rebuilding process. We continuously

With the chief of Peraliya, A. P. Darmedesa

emphasized that we were not there to take over their village, but to work together with them to get them back on their feet. After a time, the chief treated me like his granddaughter.

In spite of our fondness for each other, the chief and I would butt heads nearly every other day, though I knew he was trying to help his village in the fairest way he knew how. He never accepted any gifts for himself, always giving them away to others who needed the help more. Yet despite his equitable intentions, he would get furious when I helped certain villagers who he considered to be murderers, thieves, or whores. I explained that I wanted to take care of all people equally, just like he did. If we helped only the "good" people, then the "bad" people would be even more desperate and worse off than before. Besides, who was I to decide who was good and who was bad. I told the chief that we should leave that role up to Buddha or God.

We would hear daily reports of orphaned tsunami children being kidnapped. Two French nurses who had just joined us had witnessed a child being dragged away screaming in another area but couldn't do anything about it because the men produced Sinhalese paperwork. In Sri Lanka, when orphaned children reached a certain age, they often were sent to work for free in rich people's homes or sold as sex slaves through the human trafficking markets. Thailand, Sri Lanka, and other nearby countries were the biggest sellers of children in the world. But we weren't going to let it happen on our watch. So Bruce and James, a journalist volunteer from London, took a digital photo of every child in our village and drove inland to have them printed into school identification badges. The kids wore them every day. We kept an eye on everyone who came and went from Peraliya, and even put a guard at the hospital door and created patient cards for those who entered the hospital.

During our first week in Peraliya, the Sri Lankan trade and commerce minister, Mr. Jerarj Fernandoupulle, visited our camp to examine the tsunami damage. He said that he had been all over the country and that this was the worst area. He inspected our camp and then sat talking with us in our fly-infested hospital. Jerarj said he was impressed with our camp structure and gave us his blessing to continue running the show. He then gave us his private cellphone number and told us to call him if we needed anything. If things got stuck in customs, one call to Jerarj and the problem would be solved. Oscar loved the guy and referred to Jerarj as our godfather. The minister even assigned policemen to the village, saying they would watch over the villagers and the volunteers. Jerarj was a great man who crossed the line from official to volunteer. Throughout our time in Peraliya, he made regular trips to the village, which we always appreciated.

Every day, I would be greeted by cats and dogs that jumped all over me, anxious for a feed. Pregnant cats walked around with no food in their tummies and puppies looked like walking skeletons. They were my new friends, yet they were slowly starving to death. Each morning, I would stop on the way to the village to get them food, and I'd administer eye drops to the cats that had lost their eyes.

In that part of the world, animals were typically beaten to death by rocks and treated atrociously. I once came across a small child who had kicked a puppy to death just for the fun of it. The locals had behaved that way for generations; it was nothing new to them. But I loved and fed the animals, and soon I had a tribe of loyal subjects following me everywhere. Some of the dogs were vicious junkyard animals that had been beaten by people their whole lives. All they needed was a kind, loving hand, and soon they were purring at my side like kittens. They became great guard dogs, too, since nobody would dare go near them.

One shaggy dog in particular stole my heart. I named her "Tsunami" at first, but that didn't turn out very well. Every time I called her, the villagers would start running in fear. I changed her name to Tsunami-dog, spoken really fast. She was possibly the sickest being I had ever come across. When we met, Tsunami-dog was extremely underweight and had mange, worms, parasites, bleeding ears, fleas, and just about every other thing wrong with her. But once you got past the revolting exterior, she had a perky personality, and we grew more in love every day. She had a permanent smile on her face. I located a vet to give her injections, and her coat slowly grew back. Soon, she was even cute.

Tsunami-dog followed me everywhere, not just for food but also for companionship. We went for walks on the beach and cuddled in front of the hospital, and she spent many hours humping my leg. At night, when I left Peraliya, she would run after my motorbike. In the morning, she was there to greet me at the front gate. She loved me unconditionally.

However, I often wondered if she would have been better off without me because after I had cleaned her up, she became quite the village tart. Every dog in the village wanted to have sex with her, leading to many difficult pregnancies.

Upon awakening one morning, I noticed that one of my kittens was missing. I found out that some of the villagers had cooked her up in a pot for dinner. This wasn't customary, but they were very hungry. The village people had no food or money and were too scared to go back onto the ocean to fish. Clearly the food we were providing wasn't enough. Earlier on in my emails, I had prayed for angels to come help us. Now I prayed for everyone in the world to come to our village.

In late January, James the journalist from London set up a volunteer website called Peraliya.com where we challenged people from around the world to come and help us in the village. We didn't have time for detailed instructions, so at the top of the page I wrote, "Just come! We need your help. Get on a plane and drive to our village. Everyone is welcome here!!" And they came. Volunteers of every type from all walks of life and many different countries just showed up in Peraliya, and, as promised, we found a place for each one.

James had become a valuable member of the team. He was a highly intelligent Englishman with a great sense of humor. He charmed all the female volunteers, which in turn kept up morale. He was always thinking of new ideas to improve the village life. One day he came up with a plan to delouse the children, which was a mammoth task. They used balloons and tricks to set about coaxing the children toward the water buckets. The children laughed and screamed, and after much drama, a lice-free victory was the hairdo of the day.

Our volunteers included CEOs and businesspeople, housewives from London, actors, teachers, lawyers, writers, surfers from Sweden, and even a stripper from Paris. Many people would declare that they had no skills, but we would tell them to do whatever they felt like doing, and it worked. We would see those same insecure volunteers playing with the children or contributing in other ways, building structures out of rubbish, cooking, acting as assistants in the clinic, or just cleaning up. One man with obsessive-compulsive disorder turned out to be the best person imaginable to have in a fly-infested hospital.

All of us volunteers would laugh about some of the cultural stereotypes that proved to be true. The Germans were very organized and had a lot of money. They had rules and strong ideas about leadership, but their hearts were in the right place. The Austrians were laid back, tech-savvy, and had a great sense of humor. The Italians brought stylish tents and good red wine.

Then there were those who busted stereotypes. Kym Anthony, a CEO from the largest bank in Canada, brought his eighteen-year-old daughter, Callen, with him because it was her birthday wish to come and help. They lowered their heads in manual labor and had an overwhelmingly positive family experience.

There was a cool English couple named Jo and Rob who were only twenty years old and on their way around the world when they stopped to volunteer for five months. Some days they would peel carrots, and on other days they'd collect bodies, build, and take on just about every task imaginable. Rob then encouraged his entire family to come over. His amazing father, Peter Nossitor, a builder with J. G. Gleeson, went on to bring over many of his co-workers as well as other family members.

The beauty of volunteering is that you don't need any skills to give someone a hug or hand out water. Anyone can do it. People think that after a disaster only medical or construction help is needed, but there are also thousands of traumatized children sitting around, and they need friends, entertainers, educators, and mums and dads as much as medical and financial help.

As more volunteers joined us, the town became busier and our guesthouse noisier. Each night back at the guesthouse, volunteers would show off their daily war wounds of bruises and scrapes. The volunteer medics were constantly digging splinters and nails out from everyone's feet. Volunteers looked scruffy, sunburned, unshaven, and uncombed, but they had gigantic smiles on their faces.

The volunteers were able to buy a new wardrobe in the street markets for under a dollar. Many of the men started wearing saris on their bottom halves just like the Sri Lankan men. The sari was the national dress code of Sri Lanka and in the coastal villages we seldom saw men in pants.

Most volunteers came and went within a week and had few responsibilities, so they stayed up late at night on the beach letting off steam and playing guitars around a blazing fire. A few of the surfer volunteers would disappear whenever the surf was up, but they always came back. The mixture of work and play kept them balanced. Many romances blossomed. Volunteers often had to use hand signals to communicate with one another because they didn't speak the same language, but it didn't stop them from making love. Bruce was our number one quiet achiever. Many volunteer girls had crushes on him. Oscar and I had already been a couple for some time, so at night we usually just ate dinner and went to sleep exhausted from the day. Donny remained loyal to his family back home in Australia. He was exhausted every night, getting up at five each morning to work in the melting sun. The only fluid he was getting enough of was beer, which relaxed him into a deep sleep every night.

We did manage to have some fun, too, in the midst of all our hard work. Oscar's birthday was in late January, so we decided to have a celebration on the beach near our guesthouse with all the volunteers. We located long wooden tables and decorated them with local flowers and candles. Then we sat down to a delicious meal prepared by a local guesthouse. We ate fresh fish, fruit, rice, and dahl, and the local Lion beer flowed.

Later, the chief and a group of fishermen from Peraliya showed up. They joined in the celebration, and we realized that it was the first time we had hung out together socially. The Sri Lankans couldn't hold their liquor so they got really drunk and the chief started dancing in a kind of disco-robot manner around the fire. I joined him, and we had a *Pulp Fiction* moment. The village men serenaded Oscar with drums, then asked him to sing for them. He howled "O Sole Mio" in an unknown key, and the dogs joined in.

Then the chief pulled out a large joint and the peace pipe was handed around to all who cared to partake. The sky was painted silver and I relaxed against a coconut tree into the enchanted night. Some of the German and Dutch guys got naked and went for a moonlit swim, while one of them took off on a motorbike with an Israeli girl to a secret island destination. It was a great night and friendships among locals and volunteers bloomed.

On January 26, we held a memorial service for the one-month anniversary of the tsunami. It also happened to be *Poya*, a Sri Lankan holiday celebrating the full moon, which was marked by a Buddhist ceremony in which the whole village stays up the entire night chanting prayers. Elegantly costumed male dancers led a drum procession to a staging area where people sat on the ground. Monks presided over the ceremony, sitting in a specially woven grass hut.

It was both a spiritual and a spooky night. Most of the Buddha statues had been beheaded during the tsunami. The villagers adorned the headless statues with flowers and surrounded them with candles, praying at their feet. Oscar, Bruce, Donny, and I walked around the village visiting families and lighting candles to honor the dead. The train tracks were sprinkled with oil lamps and candles were placed inside. I lit some candles in the rubble of Chamilla's house and a few young children held back my hair when I came too close to the fire.

In Sri Lanka, the monks were revered. Whenever they came to visit, it was a rule that a villager had to place a white sheet on the chair before the monk could sit down. I hadn't learned this rule, so during the ceremony I casually went over and sat on one of the comfortable white chairs, thinking they were for us. Some village men grumbled at me in disgust and pointed for me to sit on the dirt floor.

The Peraliya monks were honest, kind, and very young. Some of them were still kids. It was difficult for them to preside over tsunami funeral ceremonies where people had lost over eighteen family members. The young monks' voices would weaken at times during the ceremony and they would burst into uncontrollable tears. I had spent time with many monks in Burma and Thailand, but this was the first time I had ever seen them cry in public.

The *Poya* chanting was soothing and rhythmic. I found it impressive for the first few hours, but then it began to put me to sleep. I noticed the other volunteers nodding off, too, so we headed back to our guesthouse in Hikkaduwa. When we got back there, we could still hear the chanting, which was being broadcast through the entire town by loudspeakers. By now it annoyed us, sounding whiny and repetitive and continuing all night long. Some of the volunteers threw objects at the loudspeaker in the tree, screaming profanities out their windows, but the chanting kept on.

Life in Peraliya sped along, and soon it was February. Every day, hundreds of bored children would hang out around the hospital. They had no homes to go back to. We realized that it was time to reopen the school. It was important to get the kids back to some sort of normalcy and give them something to do during the day.

Ironically, the villager who was most resistant to the idea was the headmaster. He was a cowardly, weak, lazy man from another region and he fought against any reasonably good ideas presented to him. Another problem was that the teachers themselves were tsunami victims and many were still traumatized and getting their own lives back together. However, we knew that reopening the school was the best thing to do for the children. So we held a village vote, and the majority of locals gave the plan their approval.

Oscar, Bruce, and James started by building a small open classroom at the end of our makeshift hospital. They weren't construction workers, so they made it up as they went along. They found large planks of wood and canvas to rig a shelter from the sun. James had originally come to help only for a day, but when Oscar thrust a hammer into his hand and asked him to finish building the classroom, he said that he was willing. When it was finished, they had matching thumb blisters in exactly the same place and were proud of themselves. Two female Dutch volunteers gave English and art lessons in the open classroom, and the children were kept busy learning all types of ideas from the Western world.

Meanwhile, Geoff Fischer, a sixty-eight-year-old Irishman who had come to volunteer for six months, led the charge on rebuilding the permanent classrooms. He had been involved with the unions back home and was a tough, strong man. He was unusually fit for his age and never wore a shirt. The local teenage boys thought he was gay, and they taunted him and whistled at him when he passed by, which pissed him off to the point of wanting to beat them up. We found it extremely funny but tried to keep a straight face as he vented his frustrations to us.

A local woman named Deebeka donated school uniforms, books, and pencils for every child enrolled in school. She had saved up to go on a holiday to Germany, but instead used her money to pay for these generous gifts.

The opening of the school approached, but one major problem remained: A quarter of the villagers were still sleeping inside the building at night. So we had to get there early in the morning, pack up the mattresses, and prepare the school for the opening day. Somehow it all came together, and seeing those beautiful children glowing in their white uniforms with huge smiles caused major tears of joy to leak down my face. It had been a difficult job but we had pulled it off.

The monks of the village performed a blessing of the school that seemed to last for days, chanting on and on in their sacred maroon robes. The children sang Sri Lankan songs in the local language of Sinhalese and everyone was in a great mood. The teachers showed up, too. They just watched the kids all day without teaching, but it was a start.

I had my video camera with me and pointed it toward the children in their new uniforms. They jumped up and down in excitement in front of the camera. I thought they were telling me about their first day at school, but much later I had the footage translated and I was horrified to discover what they'd actually been saying. One child was telling me that he had lost his mother, father, four sisters, and his grandmother in the tsunami, and was excited about being on the news and in the newspapers. Another was trying to tell me about her school friends and teachers who had died.

Oscar and I had planned a surprise for opening day. We changed into adult-sized replicas of the children's school uniforms, which Deebeka had made for us. We wore our outfits proudly, skipping around the school grounds holding hands and visiting all the classrooms, to the delighted screams of the children. The smiles stayed etched on our faces for days.

Even after we reopened the school, there wasn't enough space for all the kids. Most of the older children still met in large, white, stinking-hot tents. In each tent, sixty noisy children crowded together. The field hospital had become so overcrowded that many of the children wouldn't stand in line to get help. So I would go from tent to tent examining each child's legs, looking for infection. I would line up the students who needed medical attention outside the tents and then march them over to the hospital. The lines doubled as naughty but healthy boys snuck to the end of the line in order to get out of school. This was familiar territory to me—I had been a math teacher in Australia for six years and was ready for their tricks. I even had a few of my own.

During that first week of school, the British and German Interpol came through Peraliya looking for missing tourists in the hopes that they could return the bodies to their families abroad. But their way of doing it was offensive: They just dug up the graves, which had thousands of rotting bodies in them. Bulldozers played a round of polo with the bodies and then after a day of these Olympics, they simply dumped the corpses back into the pit and pushed sand over them. With the opening of the graves came a nauseating smell, which blasted through the village for days. It was so bad that each schoolchild had to wear a face mask in the classroom.

One day, when more than 600 children were gathered for an assembly, a local man ran through the village yelling, "Tsunami! Tsunami!" The scene that followed mimicked what it would have been like on that fateful day had people known what was coming. Children with sheer terror on their faces ran screaming in all directions. Everyone except the volunteers was in a panic. It was shocking to witness, and afterward it took us days to coax some of the children back to school from the safety of the jungles. It helped to have Oscar leading the way on a motorbike with a handful of candy.

The fisherman who had cried wolf had been drunk at the time. He assured us that he had been convinced a real tsunami was coming. But Oscar was furious with him and took him into a back room that served as a temporary jail, threatening a five-year sentence. The chief and Donny secretly freed the man after he'd spent a few hours in the makeshift jail cell, much to the relief of his family.

Oscar's overreaction to the incident, unfortunately, was becoming more typical of his behavior. Running a village proved to be quite a power trip for him, and he later joked that he had turned into Mussolini for a while. The hard work took its toll on me, too, and on our intimate relationship as well. I gave out so much love in the village that by the time I got back to the guest-house every night, I had nothing left to give to Oscar. I felt like a tube of toothpaste whose love had been completely squeezed out.

CHAPTER 6

By March, I had settled into a routine of waking up to a pot of tea and fresh papayas for breakfast. Then I would walk down to the beach to play with the stray dogs before heading into Peraliya.

Every day held new challenges, and with no sign of additional aid money arriving in our region, Oscar, Bruce, Donny, and I agreed to stay on indefinitely in Sri Lanka. We simply felt that we could not leave these people while they were still in so much need. I knew that my landlord in New York would be freaking out about my unpaid rent, but I felt the situation in this part of the world was far more important than my rent back home.

James and Juliet, another British journalist, started a fun photography class after school. Many people passing through the village loved taking photos of the kids, and we had often joked that we should arm the children with cameras to start taking photos of the visitors instead. James and Juliet turned the joke into reality. They gave cheap donated cameras to the children and provided extensive lessons on how to use them. They hoped that having the young people document their own family and tsunami experiences would lead to some healing.

The photos proved to be very interesting, so James and Juliet created an art gallery in a broken-down house. The villagers never visited, but the volunteers did. I asked a child about his out-of-focus photo, which looked to me like a simple image of the blue sea. His response was quiet and direct: He told me it was the ocean that had brought the great tsunami, which had washed away his family.

At all hours of the day and night, Donny would find hurt people along the roadside and call me to open the hospital to help them. Donny and Sebastian once came across a very bad tuk-tuk accident where a man lay bleeding to death. They couldn't get him help in time, and the man died in their arms. Donny was never the same after that incident. He and Sebastian both cried into their beers all night.

On March 29, at approximately 10:30 p.m., we received a text from James, who had recently returned home to England. The message read: "Huge earthquake/tsunami warning/head to higher ground now!!!" Our hearts raced. The death toll from the December tsunami had now risen to a horrifying quarter of a million people, and we had seen how people had reacted to the Fisherman Who Cried Wolf, so we knew that a new warning would send them running in sheer panic. We were faced with a dilemma: save ourselves, or go to Peraliya and warn our new family of over 3,000 people of the coming danger? It was an obvious decision for us; we chose to warn everyone.

I looked around my room wondering what to save, but no

material possessions meant anything to me at that moment. I grabbed my passport, flashlights, and my night vision goggles. I looked briefly out into the blackened sea and wondered what was coming toward us. Oscar and I then ran around Hikkaduwa, warning the other volunteers and hotel owners. The news traveled rapidly in a chain reaction.

We quickly jumped onto our motorbike and headed over to Peraliya. A mass evacuation was already under way. People fled on foot, carrying their babies and young children the three miles inland. We met up with the village chief, who seemed to have things under control. He was organizing the men, who had wrapped ropes around their bodies so that they could climb coconut trees and tie themselves on in case a tsunami came through. They were ready to conquer the unknown darkness of the sea. One of the men, who had lost his whole family in the last tsunami, yelled, "Come and get us, we are ready! You are not stealing any more of our babies!" He screamed like a madman, holding the rope tightly in one hand and a machete defiantly in the other.

As we followed the stream of people inland on our motorbike, villagers called out to us for help, but there was nothing we could do. We felt blind to what was coming. James in the United Kingdom was our only link to the outside world, closely monitoring the situation and keeping us updated as best he could via text messages. We urged the villagers to keep heading inland.

Eventually we found our way up a steep hill. There, at a school located a few thousand coconut trees away from the sea, the women and children gathered. The women rushed at me when we arrived, speaking all at once, weeping in Sinhalese while pushing their children into my arms. "Please save my babies," they cried. "I have lost eight and I have only this one left." I reassured them that they were safe here.

I closed my eyes to summon the angels I had asked for at the beginning of January. In the office, I found a basic stereo system and a few old cassette tapes, so I was able to play some classical music through the loudspeakers to calm the crowds. A villager had brought biscuits and water, which we passed around while making small talk. Many pregnant women had run inland with other children on their hips. I sat down to comfort them.

The hours trembled by. Then James gave us word from the BBC that no wave was coming to swallow us after all. Some people started slowly heading back to their homes, but others stayed inland just to be sure. Back at the Peraliya beach, Oscar and I sat with the chief and fifteen village men watching the ocean through my night vision goggles. The moon was full and soft waves licked the shoreline. The dogs sat with us, which was a good sign; during the tsunami, they had been the first to leave. The villagers had noted that humankind was too busy walking around with its noses in the air to read the warnings from the earth. The animals, on the other hand, had their noses low to the ground and felt the earth vibrate, alerting them to run to safety.

Oscar and I agreed that it had been better for us to be safe than sorry. We hadn't wanted to be responsible for not raising the alarm. These people had become our brothers and sisters, our blood, and we would put ourselves between the wave and them any day. Now we just had to find them and coax them back home.

Later, I found out that thirteen people had died that night running away from the tsunami scare. It filled my soul with pain. I started thinking about how the region desperately needed some sort of tsunami warning system.

The very next day, I came up with an idea. The village had no communications devices—no radios, TVs, phone lines, or anything. I realized that if there were just some sort of communications center that could get the latest information, it could spread word of tsunami warnings and false scares throughout the region. I began collecting money from my parents and friends to buy small wireless radios for every family in the surrounding villages.

Bruce had found a medical intern working at a Colombo hospital, Dr. Novil, who agreed to come help us at our clinic in Peraliya. A shy, humble man, he always put others before himself. He would work long hours during the week at his hospital, and then take a four-hour bus ride to work in our health clinic on weekends.

After the night of the tsunami scare, Dr. Novil also recognized the need for a village tsunami warning system. We discussed our ideas, and he drew up some basic plans on paper for using speakers connected through wires to the village. We decided that our center should be located in the only privately owned building left standing in the village—a two-story house right across the road from the ocean. The idea was for this center to be manned by villagers on a rotating schedule. We then organized a village meeting to discuss plans for the tsunami warning system. We were pleased when the villagers showed a strong interest in the project.

Over 250,000 people were killed during the 2004 Asian tsunami; around 40,000 of them were in Sri Lanka, and many of those were in our area. There were still so many bodies left lying around that they turned up every day during the rebuilding process and regularly washed up on the beach. It was critical to clean them up, both for hygienic reasons and to help people recover psychologically from the disaster. No one wants to run into a human body part while crossing a field, and people were looking for closure by finding the bodies of their loved ones. We felt it was important not to leave any body part behind. Right after the disaster, the police had been actively involved in the tsunami body recoveries, but eventually they grew tired and gave up. So I decided to take matters into my own hands.

In my first weeks in Peraliya, I had collected bodies using body bags that German paramedics had given us. But when those ran out, I used green garbage bags and old shopping bags. I was constantly on the lookout for new body bags and called the Navy, the Air Force, and the Army asking for donations, but Sri Lanka was completely out of bags. My cousin Christine ordered some from Australia but they never arrived, so another volunteer brought us chic designer body bags from Paris.

I usually went to collect bodies alone or with one or two volunteers, but for our first large body collection expedition, I gathered up a dozen or so volunteers and headed inland, where the water had surged up a river and taken hundreds of villagers along with it. We trekked for miles with sweat pouring down our faces and backs. The German paramedics who walked with us were dressed in hospital whites, which quickly became covered in sweat and dirt.

We came to an exposed area where I saw something strange lying in front of me. At first I didn't recognize it. It was a human body with two feet sticking up in the air. Everyone took two steps backward as I walked over to it. The toes were long and elegant, the feet dry like someone had drained the water out of them. The lower legs barely had any meat left on them, but the thighs,

Body collecting

chest, and inner organs were still in good condition. The head was a raw skull with long black hair caressing it. I stared at it, knowing that sooner or later I would have to pick it up. This, after all, was the reason we had come.

I slipped oversized blue rubber gloves over my hands and unzipped the white body bag, placing it next to the body. Then I quickly picked up the legs and swung them into the bag, followed by the heavy head. I zipped the body bag up, trapping the flies and maggots inside. One of the paramedics helped me carry the corpse to our designated collection spot. Donny came walking over from another direction with his own body bag, his face looking drained.

The second body I found was not far from the first, but it was stuck in a soggy, muddy place and a lot harder to unearth. I was wearing the black Army boots that I had purchased in Soho only a few days before leaving for Sri Lanka, which felt like a lifetime ago. I craved a bubble bath and my Jimmy Choos, but instead here I was, digging up corpses under a sweltering sun.

I found a long wooden plank and placed it in the mud in front of me so that I could walk out to the body without sinking into the mud. When I reached the body, I squatted down and gave a solid tug on the head, which snapped off into my hands. The rest of the body fell back into the swampland. I found a huge stick to lift the stringy legs over to my body bag, but then the thighs snapped off. "Pass me that leg," I said to a hippie volunteer who had come to help me. In a Sri Lankan minute (which means a long time), the dirty deed was done.

The grim operation went on for hours. When it was over, we headed back home in silence, swinging the bodies over our backs like a delivery of dirty clothes to the laundromat. Once we were out of the jungle, we collapsed in exhaustion and drank king co-conuts under a palm tree. Donny threw up. He said it hadn't been the sight of the dead bodies as much as the revolting smell of decay that had disagreed with him. This is where my Chanel No. 5 came in handy. A little under the nose took me all the way to Paris. *Vive Coco Chanel!*

In some villages, more than forty children and adults would watch our every move as we collected bodies. Some trips would generate twenty-four corpses, others just one or two. The bodies had millions of maggots and flies living inside of them and were mostly unrecognizable to their loved ones. I became fascinated with the bodies in their various stages of decay. They turned up in trees and drains and under rubble. Oscar came with us once, but he fell into a mud hole filled with bodies up to his waist. After that experience, he never came again. On one occasion, I found a body in a strange location at the very top of a steep hill where no water could have possibly reached. I wondered if it could have been a murder.

Several weeks and many body collections later, I became known as the Body Collector. People started bringing me unidentified heads and legs and other body parts. One afternoon while I was sitting on the side of a dirt road with a tattered leather bag full of legs and arms hanging out of it, a little boy ran up to me and handed me an arm. I laughed out loud as I made room in my bag for it. I had to stash body parts in the school's new bathrooms and other sneaky places at night to keep the dogs from eating them until the coroner came the next day to retrieve them.

I am not usually a superstitious person. Yet I couldn't help but notice that on numerous occasions during those first few weeks of body collecting, Oscar's motorbike would stop running for no reason at all at the very same spot on the road to Peraliya. There was nothing wrong with the bike and it was always full of gas; it felt as though something was drawing us to the area. A week later while out collecting corpses, I found a woman's body in a beautiful sea-blue dress close to where the bike had stopped each time. The body was three feet underground, hidden by a tree trunk, and covered with sand. A small piece of the blue dress sticking out of the sand had caught my attention. After I collected the body, Oscar's bike never stopped there again.

In mid-April, we arrived in Peraliya one day to find the ocean flooding into the tents and temporary wooden shelters. A large tide was seeping in. The tsunami had taken along with it an extra four feet of earth and destroyed the drainage system, so half of the village was now underwater. The highway had flooded, too, and traffic had backed up along the coast.

Donny took charge, stopping bulldozers along the road to help create a wall of rubble to block the sea. I walked around the village in gumboots, visiting families in their huts. In some areas the water came up to my waist, and we hurried to save beds and blankets. Sacks of rice were ruined, as was much of what the villagers had carefully collected for the past four months.

The sea continued to rise. Oscar and Bruce set up wooden tide markers behind the village to judge the water levels surging up the river. We needed new shelter fast. Amazingly, earlier in the day I had placed a business card in my pocket, given to me by a man I had smiled at in town. He was from the Salvation Army. I called him and told him that I needed forty tents right away. He indicated that they would arrive in a few hours, and he was as good as his word. We set the Salvation Army tents on higher ground. Soon the tidewaters receded, and our latest crisis was averted.

Peraliya had become a well-known IDP camp. Our hard work had earned us a good reputation along the coast and in the Sri Lankan newspapers. The villagers and the Sri Lankan papers had given me the title "Angel of Galle," and people came from all over the country to meet me. It was quite a silly title, but sometimes it proved useful. One man traveled nine hours on a bus to meet me, bringing one pineapple with him to give to the village. When he told me he was a rich farmer, I sent him home to bring us back a truckload of fruit. He returned days later with mountains of tangy sweet pineapples. If the Angel nickname was going to help us move forward, I'd take it.

We had heard in the news reports that billions of dollars in tsunami aid money had been collected around the world. It was one of the largest fund-raisers recorded in history. But the money hadn't reached Sri Lanka. Our project in Peraliya survived initially off our own money and funds sent to us from friends and family through Western Union, and later with donations from other volunteers and people who found out about us from friends and sent money over the Internet. My friends Melinda Roy and Taylor Poarch, for example, collected money from friends in Florida and from the dancers of the New York City Ballet to help us.

But the four of us were broke. We hadn't paid our hotel or food bills in Hikkaduwa in months, and I was now behind in rent on my apartment back in New York, too. Then an angel from Texas named Larry Buck crossed our path. A minister, he had come with funds from his church to help the tsunami victims, as well as with a group of Philippine medics and some fishing boats. When he asked us what we needed, we answered as we always did, by requesting something for the village. But Larry stopped us from speaking and asked us what we needed for ourselves. We never accepted anything but food, so we told him we were fine. On arriving back at our guesthouse that night, we found that Larry Buck had completely taken care of our room and food bills.

CHAPTER 7

The villagers in Peraliya had also heard about all the international aid money raised and started wondering what had happened to it. They began accusing one another of having it and not sharing it. Inevitably, their accusations turned to us. We tried not to give money out in front of people and would usually spend it on goods for the village as a whole rather than on individuals. But every now and again, a story would break my heart and I would quietly slip a few dollars into someone's pocket for a pair of eyeglasses or heart medication. By the time I had walked back to the hospital, the rumors would already be buzzing that I had given away $10,000.

Whenever we gave out free goods, such as clothing, it caused a lot of trouble. The women would line up in the hot sun for hours while the village men sat under the coconut trees drinking *arrack*. The women would sometimes get aggressive, pushing one another to be first in line and then fighting over the goods, often ripping the donations in half. When I ran out of clothes to give away, sometimes they would spit on me.

On one occasion, I had only forty-five mosquito nets but more than 300 women waiting. Everyone wanted a mosquito net, and when there were no more left, the women attacked, scratching and bruising me. I had had enough of their bickering and jealousy, and I wanted to show them how disgusting their behavior looked. So I started screaming like a wildcat, swinging my arms out in front of me with sharp nails clawing into the air.

The women stopped in shock. There was a quiet pause followed by great howls of laughter when they realized I was mimicking them. The group dissolved in shame . . . only to start right back up again the next day. I made the decision then that I wasn't going to be the one to physically give out aid anymore; someone crazier than me would have to deal with that hell.

The adults were behaving like children and the children were behaving like adults. When asked if they had received food that day, the adults would lie and say no, just so they could get more free stuff. We learned to ask the children first because they always told us the truth. Sometimes when the villagers complained too much at the clinic, I would lock the door and walk away down the railway tracks. The children would run after me surrounding me with love, telling me that I was helping them and that the grown-ups were bad. They would all try to kiss me at once, which melted my soul, and I would walk back to the hospital for business as usual.

Somewhere in the growing-up process, we lose our way and become too complicated. We teach our children not to fight and to love one another but we don't do that in our own adult lives. I learned a great deal from the children in Peraliya: They taught me the importance of spontaneity, the ability to pick up and move on, to adapt, to forgive, and to trust.

With Nardika (far left) and her sisters

When the weather was too rough to swim in the ocean, we paid off a local hotelier to let the kids swim in his pool during our Sunday outing. Usually it was prohibited for locals, but when no tourists were in town he agreed to it. We had so much fun swimming in the pool, but the kids would jump on top of me with their lice-ridden hair tentacles crawling all over my body, and I was terrified of catching them. I could hear those little white buggers slowly conspiring to jump on my hair. Nardika, the little girl I had helped on the first day in the village, and her teenage sisters wore their long hair in childlike plaits, but it didn't hide the white specks that lived in them. I'd grown very close to those girls, who told me that before the tsunami, their father often went hungry while giving them his share of the food and they would sing songs to his tummy when it was growling from hunger. In a way, the tsunami had been a good thing for them, because now they had food to eat. The disaster had leveled the socioeconomic playing field.

It was a miracle I never caught lice from any of the children, but something lived on my face for a while, an organism so small that it was undetectable by the human eye. In extreme heat, it would make my face itch unbearably all day long. I was determined to kill whatever it was. I scrubbed my face with alcohol, and after that failed, I tried a whole bunch of strange concoctions, including toothpaste and nail polish remover. (Warning: Do not try this at home.) The product that finally did the job was the lice-killing solution we had used on the children. I slathered it on like a face mask and let it soak in for ten minutes. It stung a little but I stuck with it, convinced that it was killing the little critters on my face. And indeed, after that I had no more itches. I must have caught it from kissing my Tsunami-dog. She had all sorts of crawly things living on her but was so cute that I couldn't resist cuddling her anyway.

Donny would rise while it was still dark out to get a head start on the day before the hot sun melted the workers. He would arrive at Peraliya way too early, waking everyone up. He would walk around the village, checking on the rebuilding progress, then stop off in one of the homes for tea. There, he could speak with small groups of men about various village problems in a casual, friendly setting. Donny was an immensely valuable member of our team and also my dear friend.

Then one day, Donny unexpectedly collapsed to the ground. Some villagers rushed him into our field hospital. His leg shook in the most unusual manner, like he had a snake crawling around inside him, and he said the spasms were painful. Shouren, a young Scottish doctor, took over, because the situation was too complex for me to handle. Shouren injected Donny with painkillers, and he fell in and out of consciousness as we carried him on a stretcher into the back of a van to rush him to a faraway hospital.

Seeing Donny lying motionless in the back of the van like that stunned everyone. Donny loved to make great entrances, and here he was making an even more dramatic exit, as the village women wailed around the van. Dr. Stein, our resident German doctor, and Dr. Novil, our Sri Lankan angel, went with him to the hospital. Michelle, a volunteer from London, also accompanied him and cared for him in the hospital every day. She became Donny's hero. The first hospital turned out to be quite unhygienic, so they continued on four hours north to the one decent hospital in Sri Lanka, in the capital city of Colombo.

The days passed quietly as we waited for word from Donny. Oscar drove up to visit him, and many of the villagers made the long bus trek up to the capital to see him as well. With one man down, I was unable to leave the village to visit. We felt his loss. We didn't realize until he was gone that he had been doing the work of ten men.

With Donny in the hospital, Oscar gone to visit him, and Bruce tending to logistics in Galle, I endured quite a few days in Peraliya when the workload became overwhelming. People flooded into the hospital with all sorts of problems and I did my best to solve whatever they threw my way. I held six different conversations at one time while sitting at the large hospital desk full of strange items, from a wooden leg to hula hoops to deworming tablets. Sometimes twenty people would swarm around me at once while another sixty waited outside to have their say. The whole time I also had to keep an eye on running the hospital as cheeky kids ran in and out looking for cricket balls, and other villagers tried to sneak supplies.

Visitors from an American Southern Baptist church had stopped by to meet me when I received a call to retrieve sixteen bodies, so I just took the guests along with me. We continued our conversation as we collected corpses (which I now looked forward to doing because it gave me a chance to get some exercise). A local chopped down some king coconuts for us, and we drank these as we hiked for miles through the rugged jungle. After we finished our task, we hitched a ride on an old tractor-trailer back to the hospital. I never saw that group again.

Inside the small kitchen located at one end of the hospital, a few volunteers were busy preparing a Thai salad with fish sauce. It smelled like dead bodies to me, so I took a whiff from my Chanel No. 5 bottle and walked outside to breathe fresh air. But I did not find any peace out there, either. Instantly, I was swarmed by children begging for the imitation treats they called ice cream—the ice-cream man had just arrived. All throughout this stampede, my beloved Tsunami-dog excitedly humped my leg.

Ten days later, Donny returned from the hospital a different man. He had decided that he needed a longer rest and that it would be his last day in the village before returning home to Australia. He hobbled around Peraliya sharing good-byes as villagers broke down in tears at the news that he was leaving.

One thing Donny had wanted to finish before he left was a shed for an old drunken man we called Grandpa. His family had thrown him out years ago, and we would find him lying on the ground with large red ants crawling inside his ears. Donny wanted to make sure the old man had a roof over his head. Donny had contacted the family and argued with them that although their father was a drunk, he was still a human being and needed to be cared for, but his pleas had fallen on deaf ears. He made Chamilla and me promise that we would take care of him. That wouldn't be hard for me because Grandpa was one of my favorite villagers. He had been my first patient in the hospital back in the early days. He would close his hands and bow in prayer whenever he saw me, and I would pretend he was a great king coming to visit me. I would put him in my hospital chair and clean out his infected eyes while he ate milk and cookies.

Donny was close to many of the families, and they begged him not to leave. They told him that we were the only gods they had seen after the tsunami. When Donny heard that, he broke down into little boy tears and explained to them that he was not a god or a superman but just a regular human being. He told them how much he missed his wife and children. He said he felt guilty that the work was only a tenth of the way finished, but he needed to go home. They told him that if it hadn't been for his work, they wouldn't have had so much as a drink of water.

Later that night on the beach we held a farewell party. Volunteers from all over the coast came by to honor the legend of Donny. He was part of what had come to be known as "the Third Wave"—the original volunteers who had arrived to help soon after the two tsunami waves had hit, destroying buildings and killing over a quarter of a million people.

People toasted and shared thoughts, and a technobeat blasted away as the village chief and I danced our butts off. Later, Oscar, Bruce, Donny, and I walked along the water's edge to say final good-byes. The moon was smiling and a hopeful breeze warmed our hearts. We laughed and wept and spoke of memories that now shaped our souls. We hugged in a tight circle as a billion

CHAPTER 8

We had been experiencing problems of all kinds, including thievery, jealously, violence, and alcoholism. But the worst crime of all was the steadily decreasing international attention to the tsunami victims as time passed and, as a consquence, the slowing down of aid money. The day after a visiting U.N. delegation had visited, hopeful that our funds and resources might increase as a result of their attention to Peraliya, the volunteers gathered into the hospital for an impromptu meeting.

People openly shared their feelings around the hospital table. The general sentiment was that we were working our guts out and nobody in the village seemed to appreciate it—or at least that's what we thought. When things are going well, people have a tendency to remain quiet, but when times are tough, people speak in hurricanes. All we had heard these past few weeks were complaints. Every day, villagers confronted us, accusing us of stealing the tsunami money, even though we had given them everything we owned, including our clothes and the last of our money.

It felt like we were running a small country and we just couldn't please everyone. Women would lie to our faces that their children had received nothing, even though we had given them food, water, shelter, medical care, schooling, uniforms, books, and a dozen other small things. They would complain and complain, but then not propose any solutions. It discouraged us.

I speculated that the villagers were emerging from the grieving stage and realizing they didn't have anything left. Depression was supplemented with anger, and the villagers increasingly showed signs of distrust toward one another and us. Arguments broke out outside the hospital daily, often resulting in stabbings. We had to sew up an extra five people a day due to knife fights. People would stab each other over a packet of cigarettes, not thinking about the long-term ramifications of their actions. Suicides were on the rise, too, as was drug use. Some days, we would find used medical needles sitting in open rubbish piles around the school area where the children played. We knew that the needles weren't from the hospital, which routinely collected hazardous medical equipment in a sealed bucket and disposed of it in town.

Sometimes I would be alone in the hospital when drunken men would violently shake the window bars and threaten to blow the place up. I knew they could do it, too, because we had found hand grenades in the rubble in the early days, and a small child had even brought one in to a volunteer. Donny had searched extensively for dangerous explosives in an attempt to clear them all away, but more could turn up at any time.

As the volunteer meeting continued, we poured out our frustrations, and the possibility was raised of our pulling out entirely. Some volunteers thought that the people of Peraliya were too spoiled by us now and that we should go elsewhere on the coast, where the villagers needed more help.

Bruce, as always, was the voice of reason. He explained that most of the problems were coming from just a few trouble-makers. We were not trying to change the villagers' lives nor did we understand their culture, he said. We had to stay focused on the bigger picture, which was giving the villagers the basic infra-structure they needed to get back on track.

At the end of the day, we decided to call a meeting with all of Peraliya to iron out problems and ask the villagers if they wanted us to close the medical center and go home. Personally, I felt it was too soon for us to leave. I knew the medical center couldn't last forever, but I also wanted to see the end of some very bad tsunami-related infections. The next day, we posted translated signs around the village asking everyone to attend. We expected about twenty people to show up, but within a few hours more than a hundred people were milling around. We placed a long table in front of the crowd and recruited an educated Sri Lankan scholar, who just happened to be passing through the village, to translate.

The talks lasted for five hours under a punishing sun. We fo-cused primarily on solving problems, from thievery, to rebuild-ing, to distribution of goods and funds. At the end, we took a vote about the future of the medical center. The villagers were one hundred percent in favor of its remaining open. Meeting ad-journed.

We were expecting a popular American clown doctor to visit Peraliya that afternoon. But after the town hall meeting, the vol-unteers were exhausted beyond belief and wanted to go home to take showers. We left the village disappointed. The clown finally arrived while we were away and ended up having a fun time with the kids. But adults need clowns as well. We were feeling so low and discouraged after the events of the past few days, even though the meeting had gone well, that we sucked up our last bit of energy and decided to join the clown and his troupe for dinner.

He wasn't at all what we had expected. He turned out not to be funny at all, but rather loud and rude. He raved madly about President Bush, oil wars, child abuse, and suicide rates, while we sat around in a quiet gloom. I ate my meal in silence until I couldn't hold back anymore. Then I told him that we were all experiencing hardships and asked if he would please talk about something positive. The clown changed his tone and began reciting a highly provocative love poem. It was clear that his painfully awkward performance was directed at me. He moved his lips around like a horse chewing hay and stared with wanton lust into my eyes. I broke his gaze and felt like throwing up. We finished the meal quickly and escaped from the depths of despair. Along the way back to our guesthouse, we agreed that he been the angriest, most depressing clown we had ever met. With that thought, we at last burst into laughter, which saved the day.

I have always believed in good and evil. At least, those were the words I used to wrap my head around what was going on in Sri Lanka. Things were "good" when we were moving forward and all was in harmony with the universe. "Evil" was anything that stopped us from accomplishing our goals, unless there was a good reason for it.

I went further and called the evil obstacles "the snake." My ideas of the serpent emerged from Bible stories I'd heard during childhood, in which the snake tempted Eve in the Garden of

Eden. The snake represents many things in different cultures, but for me, it stood for the opponent that I was determined to conquer with love. It was not a physical, slithering snake, but rather the feeling of the presence of evil.

Those days, Peraliya felt to me like the original Garden of Eden, only overrun by snakes. My fellow volunteers—who were atheists, Buddhists, Hindus, Christians, Muslims, and from other faiths—all seemed to agree that Sri Lanka held some great magnetic pull that was beyond any earthly being's control or explanation. Our highs and lows were more extreme than anything we had felt before in our lives. I battled the snake on a daily basis and it reared its head in unexpected places, from threats from former friends to talk of attacks by suicide bombers. I told the other volunteers that showing unconditional love to people who hate you confuses the hell out of them, and in the end they always give up. But that snake wrapped its scales around us at every turn. It seemed sometimes that no matter how hard I tried to show unconditional love and compassion, the snake spat its venom upon me.

Then, about four months into our journey, I experienced a major shift in my attitude. The "snake" stopped affecting me as much, and I was able to direct my focus toward the bigger picture. I realized that the tsunami was not an act of war, and that therefore the villagers had nobody to be angry at or blame for their lives having been ruined. If a woman wanted to scold me because ten of her babies were dead, then so be it. I knew she wasn't really mad at me and that I shouldn't take it personally.

It felt like I had reached a new level in my spiritual journey. Once I let go of my ego, the things people said didn't hurt me anymore. It gave me a new sense of freedom, like I had just reached outer space and was free-falling. At Ground Zero, I had conquered my fear of death. In Peraliya, I conquered my fear of evil.

For example, one day while I was working at the hospital, two villagers raced in with ghost-white faces and said that they had to speak with me at once. They explained that the head gang leader of a nearby village had threatened to kidnap me. They pleaded with me to flee the Galle region for a while and seek refuge in Colombo or even return home. Instead, I did exactly the opposite: I insisted that the villagers take me to meet this gang leader face-to-face.

The villagers and I hopped into a volunteer's car and drove to the neighboring village. We pulled over when we came upon the group of young men whom the villagers identified as the villainous gang. I picked out the guy who was clearly the leader, sitting on a tree stump with a smug look on his face. I wasn't afraid or intimidated. I was pissed off. I felt my brain switch into a tougher, New Yorker mode, totally capable of kicking ass and unwilling to put up with anyone else's garbage.

I jumped out of the car and walked over to stare directly into the gang leader's eyes. "Do you want to kidnap me?" I asked. "Here I am." He wouldn't even make eye contact, but slunk away with his buddies like the cowards they were. I never heard from or about them again.

With that incident, I earned my reputation as the Angel of Galle, someone who was not to be messed with.

Oscar and I literally hadn't had a day off in months and were showing signs of total exhaustion. When you cry at a sunset or start putting your clothes on inside out, it's time for a break. Oscar was visibly cranky all the time lately and the smallest thing would set him off. We decided we needed a few days far away from the stresses and strains of the IDP camp. A wonderful volunteer named Sir Ed Artis mentioned that he had been given a free suite at a fancy hotel in Colombo and suggested that we use it.

It was like going from a toilet to a palace. Colombo was bustling and the expensive hotels were filled with wealthy people and representatives from very large NGOs. Some of the best-funded NGOs were paying $500 a night for these five-star lodgings and parking their brand-new imported jeeps in the hotel driveways, which made me feel a bit sick. So this is where the aid money, or at least a sizable chunk of it, is going, I thought to myself.

Oscar and I settled into our room. We experienced culture shock when we turned on the taps and felt hot water pouring out of them. I ran a bubble bath and sank into heaven. That evening, Oscar and I went downstairs for dinner. On the hotel patio, we found a Sri Lankan country-western band dressed up as Texans singing John Denver and Johnny Cash covers. That was only the beginning of a bad night. We had cocktails on the veranda and our conversation quickly turned to the village. We began to feel guilty for being in the midst of such luxury when so many people were suffering. I looked at the prices on the menu and saw how the cost of one meal could support many families in Peraliya for an entire week. Foreigners wearing crocodile shirts and peach-colored pants surrounded us. We were tired and angry and we turned that anger on each other. Oscar yelled at me for no reason and I stomped upstairs to the room. He joined me later, but we still had anger in our hearts as we fell asleep.

The next day, we thought we would make the most of the beach, but the hotel's equipment had been washed away in the tsunami, so we found a taxi to take us into town to look for goggles and snorkels. We drove around in an inferno with no airconditioning for hours as the driver tried to find a dive shop. Here it was our day off, and we were spending time fuming in city traffic! We arrived back at the hotel long after lunch and immediately threw ourselves into the ocean. Snorkeling around, we discovered that the ocean bed was filled with people's clothes and household goods. It was murky and made us sad, so we didn't stay in the water after all.

We had just gone to lie out on the beach chairs when a Sri Lankan man came running up to us, waving and yelling, "Peraliya! Peraliya!" He was one of our villagers, who had come to the hotel to meet a German lady for a donation, and was thrilled to find us there. For the rest of the afternoon, he followed us like a puppy dog, talking our ears off about his family, business plans, and also a lot of nonsense, when all we wanted was to be left alone.

That night, Oscar and I were still feeling out of place. We went down to the beach restaurant for dinner but they had run out of chairs, so we stood there in front of our table for about an hour, looking ridiculous as we waited to be seated. When they finally brought chairs and came to serve us, they announced that they had run out of lobster and just about everything else on the menu. I had been looking forward to a good meal for months and this was just another roadblock on our two-day journey of supposed "rest and relaxation." We ended up in another fight about nothing. Oscar stormed off his way and I went mine. We decided to leave early the next day and head back to our village.

With Donny gone, the dynamics of the camp changed. Many of the other more experienced volunteers had left, too, though a small group of new ones arrived from time to time. Those of us who remained buckled down to continue the rebuilding process, and homes continued to pop up everywhere.

Geoff, the sixty-eight-year-old Irishman who had been working at the village for quite a while now, took over for Donny when he left. Geoff had heaps of energy, and I have never seen anyone—with the possible exception of Donny himself—work that hard in my life. He had a sad set of tools to work with, but he got stuff done and everyone respected him.

We took to holding our volunteer meetings early every morning at our guesthouse so that we could concentrate without the villagers interrupting to ask us for things. Oscar and Donny had taken great care during the initial weeks to create lists of all the families in Peraliya, specifying how many members each one had, if there were any pregnant women, young children, or elderly people, and if they had special needs, such as a deceased primary provider or disabled person. Over breakfast, we reviewed what supplies had come in—such as temporary or permanent shelters, food, clothing, household goods, school uniforms for children, boats for fishermen, sewing machines for tailors, and so on—and looked over the list of families. We discussed problems and agreed on which families would receive what donations. It was important to make certain that families didn't double-dip, claiming not to have received aid when they had, and also to ensure an equitable distribution of goods. We were very concerned about not leaving anyone behind during the rebuilding process.

Hospital work consumed me, but I was also being pulled down the road to another village where my cousin Christine, who had come from Australia to volunteer, had decided to start a women's clinic with my assistance. That village, only a few miles down the coast from Peraliya, hadn't had much help. Christine and the villagers worked hard to clean up a ruined house to use as their center, where Christine spent every day nursing wounds. The clinic was now more than 300 women strong. They enjoyed sitting around a big pot of tea and talking about life.

Christine also came up with the idea of holding laughing classes at her clinic. She is generally a little spunky, but watching her teach a laughing class in Sydney had to have been the silliest thing I had ever seen. The people stood around in a circle and forced themselves to laugh continuously, making funny faces. Her classes were quite successful in Sydney, but when she tried to laugh hysterically in front of a few hundred village women, they just didn't understand the concept. They looked embarrassed for her and didn't know how to react. After a while, they started laughing—at her, not with her, but at least they were laughing.

Bruce was involved in planting thousands of new baby coconut trees, but someone kept digging them up again at night, undoing all of his hard work. This went on for a few mornings. When the villagers found the culprit, Bruce confronted the drunken man and we braced for the first glimpse of his anger. We had never seen Bruce get mad, and we were all dying to see him lose it at least once just to prove that he was human. He yelled to the man in a loud, firm voice, "Are you the man who has been digging up the new coconut trees?" He repeated the question loudly a few more times, walking steadily closer to the drunk. When the man finally answered yes, we thought it would surely be the juicy moment we'd been waiting for. But Bruce lowered his voice and said very softly, "Don't do that. . . . These trees are for you. Don't dig up your trees. They are for your families." The drunk man explained that he thought when the plantings grew into larger trees, the coconuts would fall on the children's heads and kill them. Bruce reasoned with him for a while, and the moment ended quietly, much to our disappointment.

Understanding what people were trying to say to us was our biggest problem as volunteers. There were three different types of translators: the ones who would translate to the best of their ability; the ones who would say they could speak English but when they didn't understand, to cover their embarrassment, would make something up that was often not even close; and the ones who would just translate something completely different from what we were saying because they wanted to help their friends and family first. We did our best to pick up words and phrases in Sinhalese, and eventually I did learn quite a bit, but not speaking the language was the most frustrating problem of the entire trip.

Sunil and Chamilla, our two main translators, were chameleons. To this day, I'm still not quite sure who they are.

Sunil was a handsome, thin Sri Lankan man in his late forties. A Canadian citizen, he had flown in a week after the tsunami to record the destruction. We met when he came wandering through Peraliya with a video camera, shooting footage of the debris. I asked him if he would shoot the rebuilding process for us a few hours a day, as I was too busy working in the hospital to do it myself. I knew the footage would be useful for fund-raisers and was important to record for historical purposes. There was no talk of making a documentary at that early stage, as we were just too busy to even think that far ahead. But in the back of my mind, I knew that we had to keep documenting everything and would sort out what to do with the footage later.

Over time, Sunil became our friend. At night, he would eat with the volunteers and we would laugh about funny things that had happened that day. Sunil loved to go body collecting with me and we often bonded over new discoveries of bones we had found in far-off jungle areas.

Much to his dismay, I was often forced to use Sunil as a translator, which got him into all sorts of trouble. He would try to remain objective behind the camera when the villagers talked about their problems, but they saw him as one of their own and constantly surrounded him, begging for special assistance. When he did help, he found the villagers accusing him of false things, such as stealing money or being unfair, so he stopped getting involved and remained quietly behind his camera.

For many months now, we had been receiving frequent visits from a grieving lady who had lost her daughter on the train that had been swept away by the tsunami. She lived a few hours down the coast, but made the bus trek up to Peraliya daily to see if we had found any new bodies. She had visited every morgue in Sri Lanka, inspecting thousands of corpses, looking for her daughter. I had never come across such an inconsolable woman. I tried to explain to her, as I had done with many others, that her daughter was in a beautiful place and that her spirit was watching over the woman, but I simply couldn't say it anymore. The reality was that her daughter's body was probably stuck upside down in a tree somewhere rotting away. With that thought, I burst into tears, making matters worse.

Sunil and I agreed that we had to think of a way to help this lady put an end to her miserable roaming of the countryside. Weeks earlier, Sunil and I had come across a body similar to her daughter's description in both height and dress, although we couldn't say for sure that it was her. Sunil had a piece of jawbone that he had picked up from that same area that day, to which he felt a strong connection. He spontaneously brought it home to his guesthouse, much to the disgust of his English girlfriend. (We weren't in the habit of collecting bones for keepsakes, but every once in a while my body bags would be full, so I would slip a finger or toe bone into my pocket only to forget it was there. I'd find it weeks later when looking for a pen.) Sunil and I both had strong separate instincts about that jawbone. Our feelings certainly may have arisen more from our desire to help the woman recover than from any scientific evidence, but deep inside we honestly believed the bone belonged to the missing daughter. So I suggested that we present Sunil's piece of jawbone to the grieving lady as a representation of her daughter to help her with the healing process.

The next time we saw the woman, we gave her the bone. We told her that she was to bury it in her backyard and create a shrine around it where she could pray each day to feel closer to her daughter. We said we hoped it would stop her agony from wandering the coast every day looking at dead bodies. We explained that there was a 99.9 percent chance that it wasn't her daughter's actual bone, but there was also a chance that it was and, regardless, she should treat it as a symbol. The woman followed our instructions. She buried the bone, and from that day on she had a place to grieve. Sunil and I were very pleased that our idea had worked.

Chamilla was the first person I met in Peraliya, and the only native of the village who spoke English. She worked hard as our translator and was extremely kind to everyone. She had three brothers, two of whom had lost their wives and children to the tsunami, as well as a baby of her own named Wassani. Chamilla, her baby, and I often would go for walks along the beach holding hands while Chamilla and I discussed life.

Chamilla played a critical role in the rebuilding of Peraliya, a job her fellow villagers never thanked her for. She served as our only translator for a long period of time, and we dragged her all over the place to hundreds of meetings. She became like a sister to me, which upset some of the village women, who turned on her in jealous rages. Their vengefulness grew so destructive that at one point I had to rent Chamilla a small place in Hikkaduwa, where the volunteers were staying, so that she could escape the persecution at night, but it only made the villagers' jealousy of her worse. I felt terrible about the difficult role we placed Chamilla in by asking her to be our translator. But I also gave her many gifts of friendship and financial support—everything I had to give.

While working in the hospital one day, a loud voice came bellowing through the window. "Why isn't anyone working?" the voice boomed. "Get off your butts and get back to it." It was Donny! He had returned, and we couldn't have been happier. He had gone home to rest and see his family for three weeks, but he knew the job wasn't finished, so he had come back.

Donny walked around the village hugging the monks and calling out "machan" to his friends, while small children pulled at his walking stick. The villagers rejoiced as much as we did. Donny remarked that when he was walking around his hometown, no one had cared about him, but when he came here, everyone cared. It was time for a celebration. The beers and king coconuts were on us that night.

Shortly thereafter, a Sri Lankan holiday shut down the village, so we decided to take the weekend off. Donny and Bruce came over for breakfast and we watched surfers shoot ten-foot curls. We played Frisbee and swam in the ocean. But no matter what, our conversations always turned to solving the village problems.

Our days were long and the responsibility of caring for more than 3,000 people grew heavy on our shoulders. Oscar was becoming more and more agitated by the lack of aid, and he expressed himself through his short temper. We had a visit from a gentle Australian doctor who volunteered to be his therapist. He was a wise and happy man who sat and listened to Oscar's problems as he lay on the bed. The doctor recommended that Oscar take a day off, and they decided to go snorkeling out to the reef together.

The next day, they set off swimming toward a large cluster of rocks. But the rocks were farther away than they had looked. Three-quarters of the way into the adventure, Oscar and the therapist grew weary and contemplated turning back to shore. Instead, they decided to finish swimming out to the rocks and hitch a ride back to shore on a passing boat. When they finally made it, they slumped onto the rocks and looked around for a ride, but by then the last boat had left and the ocean was very rough. Trapped between the reef and large waves, they were forced to swim the long way back to shore. The doctor struggled and then started to fail, simply too exhausted to swim any farther. Exerting every last bit of energy, Oscar dragged the doctor through the water and safely back to the beach. They sat catching their breath for some time, and then the doctor went back to his guesthouse to sleep.

We didn't see the doctor again for a few days, but when he did emerge he clearly wasn't the same man. Gone were his permanent smile and upbeat personality. A darker, depressed fellow sat before us. He told us that the swim had depleted him of critical nutrients and medications that were keeping him stable. He had a medical condition, and the swim had nearly killed him.

Oscar laid the doctor down on his bed, sat next to him with a piece of paper and pen, and began asking the therapist the same questions that he had asked Oscar a few days earlier. I had to run to the bathroom to hide my irreverent laughter. The sight of Oscar being anyone's therapist was hilarious. The next morning at breakfast Oscar declared that he knew things were bad when he ended up having his therapist as his patient.

So far, our volunteers had been excellent. They had dropped out of the sky from all over the world and we hadn't had a single problem. That was, until a sevety-five-year-old evangelical Texan man I'll call Jerry wandered into camp singing "Onward, Christian Soldiers." Jerry had obsessive-compulsive disorder, which meant that he did quite an excellent job at cleaning the hospital, but when, late one rainy night, he broke into the Peraliya village storage shed and decided to make it his home, I knew we were in trouble. We had a rule that no volunteers stayed in the village at night; we all lived in Hikkaduwa. The next morning we arrived to find Jerry walking around in front of small schoolchildren in nothing but his underwear. His clothes were hanging in the sun to dry. It was clear that we were going to have to ask him to leave the village.

Oscar, Bruce, and Donny were supposed to have the chat with Jerry, but in the end they were all too chicken, so I had to break the news to him myself. I explained that he couldn't live in the village. He responded that he would sleep across the road at the beach. I made many attempts to persuade him until I finally had to insist that he leave. He did leave, cursing my name under his breath. I had never had to do anything like that before, but I knew it had been the right thing when we heard rumors later on that he had "gotten into some trouble" with kids farther down the coast.

A team of New York Mount Sinai Medical Center students and their teachers suddenly showed up without warning, as most visitors were inclined to do. I was thrilled; I had no doubt that I could turn the hospital over to them and take a break. New Yorkers were among the most competent people I had ever met. Knowing that they'd immediately get to work, Oscar and I decided to go for a motocross bike ride for the day. We raced to the other side of Galle and began riding off the beaten track along all sorts of fun jungle trails. We found hidden Buddhist temples and spectacular views of the coast. We followed a very rough trail all the way down a steep mountain, where we discovered a tiny private beach that looked as though it had been spun from gold. It was an oasis away from the rubble. We took off our clothes and swam naked for hours in the beautiful blue sea. This, we decided, was our special hideaway paradise. Unfortunately, it was so secret that we were never able to find it again!

On my birthday, Oscar arranged for us to go to the Lighthouse Hotel near Galle for a night. The owners had given us a free room in appreciation of our hard work along the coast. Unlike our weekend at the hotel in Colombo, I didn't feel guilty this time because I desperately needed to recharge. If I didn't go, I might have had to return home to New York for a week. Also, unlike the Colombo hotel, this one wasn't far from Peraliya, so I knew that I could rush back to the village in no time if a problem arose.

At dinner, I ordered a delicious steak, but when it arrived my olfactory senses cheated me, making me think of the smell of dead bodies, and I couldn't eat it. But I had no trouble enjoying the room, which had a large four-poster bed filled with pillows. I swam into it and found Atlantis. I decided that there are times for IDP camps and there are times for an Upper East Side New York girl to enjoy a few five-star pleasures. Up until then in Sri Lanka, I hadn't allowed myself to enjoy any of the finer things in life. That night, Oscar and I slept for hours and our worry lines melted into the thousand-thread-and-still-counting sheets. My cousin Christine had recently given me a new bottle of Chanel No. 5, which I sprayed on my freshly cleaned body. After that one-night stay in the hotel, I felt as though I had had a two-week vacation. I wouldn't have to go back to the United States just yet.

CHAPTER 9

By May, life in Peraliya was beginning to feel like something out of *Lord of the Flies*. We had to watch our backs, as some villagers had nothing to do but cause trouble. Deep trauma set in and emotions ran high. Noisy drunks would tell us they had planted bombs under the hospital. In anger and jealousy, husbands were beating their wives and children. Aid was anorexic and fewer cars were stopping by the village. Many volunteers had left, so the remaining people had more jobs to cover.

Suicides also were on the rise. A sixteen-year-old boy threw himself under a passing train just outside the hospital. Miraculously, he survived with only a small hole in his side, which we treated at the hospital each day. During the tsunami, his heavyset father had been wheelchair-bound and his brothers had fought hard to save him as he bobbed up and down in the gigantic waves. They had been washed a few miles inland hanging on to his chair and had successfully rescued him.

When I went to the house to check in on the suicidal son, I found the boy's father rotting away in their roofless house. He had horrific infections and abscesses in his groin. With those conditions, it was only a matter of time before he died. But every time we placed him in a Sri Lankan hospital for special care, we would find him at home again a few days later. The hospital would release him because they needed the bed.

Shouren and Carolyn, Scottish MDs who had just started working with our clinic, cared for him, but when they left Sri Lanka, the father was placed in a hospital with strict instructions for the nurses not to release him until one of us returned to resume his care. The hospital released him anyway while we were out of the country, and he died in poverty from the infections a week later. He was the only one who got away from us. I remember his sad brown eyes watching my every move.

With houses well under construction and more help in the hospital from the Scottish doctors, I found time to walk around Peraliya most days visiting families. I had hundreds of new friends, and as I toured around, children and families would invite me into their simple homes to share their laughter and curious customs.

I got to know a little man and his wife who would cook rice and dahl for me while their giggling teenage girls played with my hair. One day, they called me inside to visit their eldest daughter, who had a special gift for me. They waited in excited anticipation as I opened the plain brown bag they had presented to me. Inside was an orange. It then dawned on me that there were no fruits or vegetables for sale anywhere nearby. The only fresh fruit that we had access to were the coconuts, papayas, and occasional mangosteens that we plucked straight from the trees. I hadn't seen an orange since New York. The mother told me that her daughter had traveled four miles into town by bike to buy it for me at the

Sunday market. It was indeed the most precious gift I had ever been given. I peeled the orange and shared it with the family.

Gaggles of children followed me everywhere, all trying to hug me as I walked. In extreme heat, they would walk beside me holding an umbrella over my head to shield me from the burning sun. They would quietly push one another aside and fight over who got to hold the umbrella. My hospital walls were filled with their drawings of the volunteers, which were generally quite accurate. But for some reason whenever they painted me, they drew me with black hair instead of blond. When I asked them why, they answered that it was because I was one of them.

We knew from the start that it was important, as volunteers, to do more than simply rebuild the infrastructure of the village ourselves. We also wanted to create jobs that would help sustain the locals' lives long after we left.

Bruce managed to secure a grant from Shell Oil, and I collected lots of small donations from my parents and New York friends. This quickly came to an amount sufficient to get several businesses up and running in Sri Lanka. So we set about facilitating the creation of all sorts of small industries: a bakery, a sawmill, a brickmaking factory, a bike repair shop, several sewing shops with weaving spindles and sewing machines, a mask shop, a candy store, a roti shop, a fishing supply store, and a turtle hatchery.

Usually, the head of a family would approach me, saying that he or she needed to start working again to support his or her family. Instead of handing them money, we would sit down with them and discuss a long-term business plan. We would put some numbers on paper and write a little contract of what was expected of them moving forward. We would then call around to volunteers and friends back home, asking if anyone wanted to help. Once the money changed hands, that was that. Sometimes the villagers would surprise me by naming their shops after me. There was an Alison's Enterprises and an Alison's Bike Shop, which was sweet but completely embarrassing.

Sunday was my favorite day of the week because it was swimming day. We had started the tradition by taking the children to the beach in Peraliya, but as the months went by, we borrowed minivans to travel farther up the coast where the surf wasn't as rough. There were around fifty children who attended the lessons regularly, most from the poorest families in the village. We were part of one big family now and some of the children's parents came along to keep an eye on them . . . and on us. We foreigners were accepted but always watched over carefully.

At the beach, we would play games and give swimming lessons. Swimming days were like summer camp, with everyone laughing and jumping all over one another. Sri Lankans don't usually swim, and learning how was a big treat for them. I noticed that some of the children were getting thinner, so after the lessons we would serve a simple lunch of vegetable fried rice. After lunch, we would sing for hours. My Sinhalese was improving, and I was able to communicate with the children. They loved teaching me new words. When my Sinhalese failed me, I would start counting and repeating the alphabet, which would unfailingly make the children burst into laughter. The other volunteers and I also taught the kids new English words and customs.

Oscar found joy in soccer, which was a way for him to release his aggression. In New York, he had led a physically active life, and whenever he would pass a field of people playing soccer he would join them. In Sri Lanka, he did the same thing. On the nights he came back from an intense soccer game, he was in a much better mood.

Over time, Oscar adopted the nearby Galle village soccer team and began coaching them. His team was talented, so he organized friendly matches with other teams, such as the visiting Canadian team and the Sri Lankan military team. Oscar found sponsors to buy his team jerseys and soccer shoes. Most of his teammates had never worn soccer shoes before, though, and halfway through the match they would kick them off and run without them. Through soccer, Oscar made many Sri Lankan friends and found great fulfillment.

On one of my rounds to the village next to ours, I came across a crippled little boy living in a shed who had a blind father and an autistic mother. The temperature inside must have been over 106 degrees. The little boy lay on a filthy makeshift bed. The infected fourth-degree burns covering his legs were wrapped in bloody bandages that stuck to his wounds. The sight of him broke my heart, and I raced back to Peraliya to find some toys and medicine to give him. I offered him a whistle to call his mother, two balloons, and a large green toy frog that spat water out of its mouth when squeezed. He responded as if all his *Poya* wishes had come true at once, and he gave me the most gleeful smile.

The boy's injuries were not directly related to the tsunami. He had been playing cricket with his friends some weeks after the disaster. He was a few miles inland at the time, chasing a ball across a huge cricket field, when he fell into a deep, hidden pit of boiling black oil. Roadworkers were using the oil to tar the roads but had left the pot of burning hot oil unattended. The boy's friends were far away on the other side of the cricket field when he disappeared from sight. He was in shock, but managed to pull himself out of hell and drag himself in the opposite direction to a nearby river to relieve his pain. There, the skin on his legs peeled right off, and he felt the fish eating away at his flesh. Next, he dragged his body over to the highway, where a bus picked him up and took him to a local hospital. He had been through a devastating experience and was now left to rot in his shed.

The mother asked me for money for food, so I handed them the only ten dollars I had left to my name, and apologized that it was such a small amount. When I inspected their food supply, I wondered where all the billions of donated aid dollars had gone. All they had was one plate of old rice with hundreds of flies hovering over it. I bit my lip and told them I would return with some more food. As I started to leave, the blind father got down on his knees and rapidly kissed my feet. I should have been used to this customary gesture of thanks, but it still embarrassed me intensely. I smiled and turned away from them, walking outside to find fresh air.

It had a ring to it: "The Hawaiians have arrived." I was out body collecting when along the street came a flock of Hawaiians in light blue scrubs and friendly smiles. They were from New Hope church in Honolulu, and their leaders were named Pastor Wayne Cordeiro and Doug Kennedy.

Timing is everything. The Hawaiians had arrived at a time

when we had nothing left to give. When a disaster strikes, there are often many first responders, but then everyone slowly goes away to work on the next disaster, so the second group of responders is essential. Pastor Wayne and the others had brought with them a donation from their church that helped save Peraliya.

I was sitting on the beach watching a perfect eight-foot barrel peel to the shore when it occurred to me that it was time to leave. I'm not sure how I knew, but I just did. The hospital was still quite busy but most of the initial tsunami infections had healed. We were mentally, physically, and emotionally exhausted, and it was time for us to go home to rest. I shared my thoughts with Oscar, Bruce, and Donny, and they agreed with me. We were all squeezed out. Oscar's and my original return plane tickets both had expired many months before, so our friend Kym Anthony generously booked our flights home. We were set to leave in a few weeks.

Now that we were going, it was time to move the hospital out of the old school library. As it had been one of the only buildings left standing after the tsunami, it had served as the main rebuilding hub of the village. It also had attracted a great deal of aid to Peraliya. But its time was over. Moving the hospital didn't mean it had to close—we were still seeing over 150 new patients a day—we just needed a more appropriate building. I searched the village for a new and improved location. Meanwhile, Dr. Stein, a German doctor who had spent a few months working at our clinic and shared my vision for creating a permanent hospital in Peraliya, flew home to raise money. Dr. Stein ended up seeing our dreams through to reality. He found not only German investors but also a great Aussie architect named Justin who agreed to build the hospital.

Moving day was bittersweet and rainy, with lightning exploding outside the hospital windows. Everyone pitched in to help move the medical supplies from the library over to our new temporary medical center. I carefully took down the children's tsunami drawings and saved them to rehang. They were historical documents just like the ones I had saved from September 11, and they, too, would have their place in history. It took a full day to move, but we felt satisfied when the work was done.

In the afternoon, Oscar and I shared a fun romantic dance in the middle of the freshly cleared old hospital building. Argentine tango had been a passion of mine ever since a beautiful Antonio Banderas look-alike taught me how to dance in an alley in Buenos Aires. At the end of our dance, Oscar plunged me backward until my hair almost touched the floor, and the villagers shrieked as if he were going to drop me. He then whipped me back up with a triple spin and a light kiss. It was a tender moment for us. We hadn't had time in the past six months for romance, and it had sometimes left me wondering about my feelings for him. The dance reminded me of why I'd fallen in love with Oscar in the first place.

I spent my last days in Peraliya making sure that the Community Tsunami Early-Warning Center could function without me. I knew that if I was leaving town I couldn't help the villagers individually anymore, but the tsunami center was something I felt everyone could benefit from far into the future. I hoped it would give the villagers of Peraliya, and eventually everyone along the Sri Lankan coast, some peace of mind and help them sleep soundly at night.

Dr. Novil and I hoped to install tsunami warning sirens all along the Sri Lankan coastline. We also wanted to have government-run tsunami-detecting buoys out in the Indian Ocean to record earthquakes and activity faster. But our main goal in the short term was simply to get the warning messages out to as many villagers in our area as possible, as quickly as possible. The CTEC building consisted of several computers connected to the Internet, which could receive tsunami warning messages from tsunami centers around the world. Our tsunami officers would pick up the signal and alert the villagers via a network of large sirens and loudspeakers strategically placed around the surrounding five villages. We had two recorded tapes to play: One announced that people should stay in their homes, as there was no tsunami danger; the second tape announced that a tsunami warning was in effect and instructed people to move to higher ground at once.

A group of villagers came with us to officially open the center, which was located just outside the entrance to Peraliya. Dr. Novil arranged for us to cut a yellow rope at the opening ceremony. We then sent out our first greeting via computer to other tsunami centers around the world. I had a corny idea to test the new officers, too. I looked out the window, then quickly turned to them and asked in a frightful voice, "Is there a tsunami coming?" They immediately got online and looked at the earthquake activity, then called the Sri Lankan Meterology Department in Colombo for confirmation. They announced there was no tsunami threat, and with that we all burst into laughter and applause. CTEC was up and running, ready to save lives!

We wanted the staff to take their positions seriously and to show up on time, so we made the tsunami officer position a paying job. We interviewed applicants from the entire Galle area and carefully selected the most responsible people. Officers wore new uniforms and followed strict protocol. We asked them to punchstamp a card every fifteen minutes to make sure they didn't fall asleep at the computer on their watch. The officers would work in five-hour shifts 365 days a year, funded by me and any donations I could find. Cronulla Rotary Club in Australia bought us a generator and supplies. Some of the CTEC officers had family members who had been killed during the tsunami, and they all felt proud to be protecting their people from future disasters.

After the CTEC opening ceremony, we walked back over to what used to be the field hospital, which we had converted temporarily into a movie theater. Chandran Rutman, a filmmaker friend of ours from Colombo, had brought by a DVD of *Finding Nemo* for us to screen. For most of the villagers, it was the first time they had ever seen moving images projected on a screen. Hundreds of children and adults sat in a trance as the magic of movieland swept over them.

One day shortly before we left, Oscar and I had just finished work and were feeling down. We were sitting on a rock watching the sunset and venting our frustrations to each other when a small boy whom we had never seen before jumped off a bus and came walking over to us. He said quietly, "I know who you are!" We asked him to join us for a king coconut. He shook our hands and said he had been observing us for a while. He told us that he wanted to thank us on behalf of the president of his country for the important work we had been doing. Dumbfounded at this random act of appreciation from such a young boy, we both spontaneously burst into tears of joy and sat there crying with him. It took a little boy of no more than nine years of age to take away all the pain of the past six months.

The original team: Bruce, me, Oscar, and Donny

Everyone in Hikkaduwa and Peraliya knew that the four of us were leaving. Word had spread as soon as Oscar, Donny, Bruce, and I had made the decision that we needed a serious rest. Since the four of us had arrived together, we agreed that we should leave together.

Donny and Bruce indicated that they wouldn't return for a while. Donny had to attend to family matters, and Bruce was about to go on a long tour with Pearl Jam. Oscar and I were in the middle of raising money for the new Peraliya School and running CTEC, so we knew that we would be back after a rest, probably within the next year, but we couldn't be sure of anything. We couldn't promise our return, and if we did indeed come back, it would be not to work in the village but to oversee larger projects. The villagers probably assumed we weren't ever coming back, as they had seen many volunteers leave, never to return. Regardless, we knew Peraliya as we had experienced it in these past six months would never be the same again.

We spent our last day in Peraliya at the beach, swimming and laughing with the children. They had been working on a song they had written for us, and a few days prior they had recorded it onto a primitive cassette tape. We sat around a bonfire listening to the song, which was titled "The Only Gods We See." The chorus repeated: "Alison, Oscar, Donny, and Bruce, these are the only gods we see." It was hard not to laugh out loud at the words and the children's voices, which sounded on tape like sad karaoke music. But the silliness of the song gave way to a flood of gratitude toward the children, who had spent many weeks creating it for us and who had always been there to raise our spirits.

For our final night, Dr. Novil organized a phenomenal farewell gathering with hundreds of villagers in attendance. The activities began with a parade of children chanting as they marched into the village temple. We lit candles and prayed to whatever gods we believed in. After the procession, we gathered in front of the old hospital. Many people, including Dr. Novil and some villagers, made good-bye speeches. The villagers presented awards with flowers and beauty queen sashes labeled with new titles they had given to us. Donny was named "the Good Shepherd of Peraliya," Oscar was named "the Visionary of Peraliya," Bruce was named "the Master of Peraliya," and I was named "the Nightingale of Peraliya." As they placed the sashes around us, the villagers presented us with a carved silver baton containing a rolled-up declaration from the village officially stating their deep gratitude for all our hard work. It was a blessed night as we said good-bye to our new family.

Before I was handed my sash, one of the village troublemakers who had spread many false rumors about us slipped an envelope into my hands. I made the mistake of quickly reading it to myself between speeches. In the letter, he expressed his disappointment at how unfair he thought it was that I hadn't distributed the antibiotics and medicines equally to everyone throughout the village and had instead stored them in the hospital. He complained about everything, including the moon. As I looked up from reading his note, they were announcing my Nightingale award. The bad man's words washed away with the joyful cheers from my many newfound friends. He was a rotten seed, and I knew in my heart that those types never grow in the end.

Following the ceremony, the chief invited our core group of volunteers over for a last supper. The night was calm, and we could see the lights of other campfires sparkling throughout Peraliya. The chief had been fishing for us since early dawn and sat around an open fire cooking up his catch. His wives and family cuddled around us as we laughed into the night. In turn, we all expressed our love for one another. We had formed unbreakable bonds over the past six months. The chief cried as he said that he was extremely sad to see us go and thanked us for saving his village. He told us that he would miss our friendship.

Then the chief presented us with silver rings formed in the shape of the island of Sri Lanka. In each ring sat a small red ruby, which was placed exactly where Peraliya is located on the Sri Lankan map. He asked us to wear the rings whenever we came to visit so that his offspring would recognize and honor us. The chief had a romantic way about him that I loved. The rings fit perfectly and served as a treasured souvenir of our unexpected adventure.

On leaving the chief's house, I found a dead snake on the railway tracks. This to me symbolized the end of a long battle with negative forces that had constantly been testing us throughout our stay. I was thankful that the snake was dead for now, but I knew it wasn't the end of him.

The next morning, in our last moments in Peraliya, Oscar, Donny, and I walked hand in hand along the railway tracks while my Tsunami-dog followed behind us. I had arranged for a village family to take care of her, giving them an ample supply of dog food, but I was still heartbroken at having to leave her behind. Bruce was too busy to come with us on our final tour. He had raced off on his bike, saying that he had to tie up loose ends at all the businesses he'd helped start. But I think he also may have been trying to avoid having to say good-bye.

Families came out from their houses and children collected behind us as we made our rounds through the village. Many of the villagers still begged for help, while others cried. Oscar had tears pouring down his face as he hugged the children. We had stayed for the children and had learned so much from them. But I was truly in an exhausted state and had nothing left to give. I also knew that it was important for the villagers to get on with their lives again without us. Eventually, we managed to tear ourselves away and climb into the van we'd hired to drive us back to Colombo for our flights home.

As our van pulled out of the village, I could see the thousands of new baby coconut trees that Bruce had planted. A lot had changed since those first days in Peraliya, when we had pulled into a scene of utter despair and destruction, wondering if there was anything we could do to help. New businesses were sprouting up everywhere. A great deal of rubble had been cleared. The villagers were no longer living in tents. The school had reopened. Our small first aid van had grown into a field hospital that in six months had treated a documented 75,000 patients. Medical people had come from all over the world to work there, and a new

With my beloved Tsunami-dog and her boyfriend

permanent hospital, led by our wonderful Dr. Stein, was under construction.

But our efforts never would have succeeded without the help of the volunteers who joined our efforts, everyday people who felt that they could make a difference and took the time to come here. No politics, no bureaucracy—they just showed up and got to work. That first night in Peraliya, I had prayed for every spare angel in the world to come to help us, and without a doubt my prayers had been answered.

Just then, I looked out the window and noticed my Tsunami-dog running after the van, panting and out of breath. I yelled for the driver to stop the van and jumped out to give her one last cuddle. Leaving her behind was one of the hardest things I have ever had to do.

CHAPTER 10

I had missed New York during my six-month stay in Sri Lanka. All I wanted when I got back was a chewy poppy seed bagel and *The New York Times.* But then I saw the newspapers at the airport newsstand: Most of them had headlines about Brad Pitt and Jennifer Aniston's breakup and no news at all about the tsunami recovery efforts. I had assumed that the papers would still be reporting on the effects of the disaster. Then Oscar and I arrived home, worn out from our thirty-two-hour journey, to discover an eviction notice on our apartment door. It stated that we needed to move out in six days. We had just helped rebuild more than 500 homes and had lost our own.

For the past five years on my way to the gym, I had passed by a gentle man named Ricky who lived on the street. I would often buy him food and fruit drinks. Sometimes I would sit in the gutter and chat with him, and we would watch the tall world pass by. After returning from Sri Lanka, I saw Ricky sitting in his usual spot in the gutter. He had a cup in front of him where passersby could put their money. I reached into my pocket to grab some quarters to give him, but found that I had nothing in my pocket. I realized right then and there, as I looked into Ricky's cup, that he actually had more money than I did. We both had a good laugh about it.

My mum sent me a few hundred dollars to live on, and Oscar and I used it sparingly for subway rides and bananas. We were too proud to ask wealthier friends to help us, as over the past months we had used up all our favors by asking for donations for Peraliya. Fortunately, my banker friend Phil offered to cover the rent and utilities for a time as a gesture of thanks for our tsunami relief work.

The whole beauty of the mission was that it had been spontaneous. In Sri Lanka, we had lived day by day and concentrated fully on the tasks of caring for the people there and rebuilding, not worrying about our troubles back home. Letting go of that fear was liberating; we knew we would only burn unnecessary energy thinking of such things. Having no money to my name was in a strange way freeing. I knew that I could always make more. I still had an unmoving faith that everything would sort itself out.

Hot water felt like such a treat to us now. Oscar kept turning the taps on and off, marveling at the water flow. But New York's opulence also made me uncomfortable. It seemed unfair that so many people were suffering when most New Yorkers were so privileged. However, my opinion on that topic flipped 180 degrees when I learned how much money the American people had donated to the tsunami cause, even if a lot of the funds never made it to Sri Lanka.

Meanwhile, Oscar was suffering from post-traumatic stress

disorder. He was not easy to deal with. We hid away in my apartment trying to make sense of the previous months, living on bananas and air.

I had accumulated a lot of footage of our tsunami rebuilding efforts, but it would have taken hundreds of hours to watch it, and when I got home I just didn't have the time or the energy. Although we had recorded our experience, we had never sat down to talk about making a documentary. I had just collected the tapes from Sunil each week and thrown them into a big steel container to protect them from the heat and humidity. The only thing on my mind now, besides the tsunami recovery effort, was getting a ton of sleep, which I did.

During our first week at home, we received a call from Kym Anthony, the CEO of the Canadian bank who had volunteered in Peraliya with his daughter Callen. He had organized a trading day during which the bankers had agreed to donate their commissions to the tsunami cause. He wanted us to attend the event, so he sent us plane tickets, and off we went. We were thrilled when Kym announced at the event that he and his traders had raised over $800,000 Canadian to rebuild the Peraliya School.

It also warmed my heart to receive an email from a CTEC officer about a week after I had returned to New York:

> Dear Alison,
>
> Two villagers came running to CTEC. They asked, "Is there a tsunami?" We checked the Internet and email to find out if there was a tsunami warning. There was no tsunami warning. We called the Met Department and asked whether there was a tsunami. They also said there wasn't. We told them not to worry. We announced through the loudspeakers and said there was no tsunami.

Next we called our team. We went through the commu-
nity and told them not to worry. They were happy about
our center and action. We are happy too.
  Bye, Chathura and Nadun.

Oscar and I started to hear from a few of the remaining volunteers in the area, with whom we were in touch via email, that rumors about us were flying in Sri Lanka. People were saying that Oscar had stolen all the tsunami money and was building homes for himself in Switzerland. Others claimed that we were on the run, hiding in coconut trees, and that when the international police had found us by shaking the trees we had dropped to the ground. After the cops had supposedly arrested us, we had been sent to the CIA for further questioning about where we had buried the tsunami money. The stories grew more and more elaborate.

We also heard reports from some volunteers who had just returned home to New York that Chamilla, our translator, was having a hard time. Now that we were gone, many of the villagers had turned on her with jealousy about how she had gotten too much help from the foreigners. They tried to involve her in the rumors about our having stolen the missing funds. I sent some of the volunteers still working in the Galle region to go check on her, and Chamilla told them that I had never helped her.

Sunil, our cameraman, was also being persecuted for being our friend. He didn't argue against any of the rumors about us, either. I understand that both he and Chamilla were trying to survive in a hostile environment, but it must have looked really bad to the villiagers when our two right-hand people, who had been with us every day, didn't stand by us. It set us up for a homecoming reunion that we would never forget.

We had been back in New York for only ten days when it became clear to Oscar and me that we had to return to Sri Lanka. There was still a lot more work to do over there and it was the only place we wanted to be. We felt rested and anxious to get back to work. I missed my precious Tsunami-dog. I missed the dusted white sands and the turquoise seas. I missed the red-ink sunsets and the smell of chicken curries. I missed the nightly lightning shows off the coast. Most of all, I missed the children who swarmed us in love. We repacked our gear, found friends to donate tickets once more, and, knowing that our rent was now being covered, headed back to the jungle.

When we arrived in Peraliya after a thirty-hour plane ride, exhausted but eager to see our friends again, we found excited villagers running out to greet us. Women who previously had been unkind to me dropped down on their knees and asked for my forgiveness. We saw no signs of the viciousness we'd heard reported. The villagers said that they were happy we had come back to help them.

But then we got our first indication that something was wrong. Although it was spectacular to see the children, some of them remained at a distance. Oscar felt confused and hurt when he waved at his favorite kids and they just looked away. Soon after, Oscar learned that some parents had spread lies about him to their children and told them not to speak to him. He was furious. Oscar didn't care about the adults' pettiness, but finding out that the children, whom he loved dearly, had turned against him sent him over the edge. He flew into a rage and dragged the local police around to the villagers' homes to clear up the stories.

Of course, each person blamed the rumors on someone else's brother's cousin's nephew, who just happened to be absent.

To leave as helpers and to return as thieves was insulting and heartbreaking. I suppose that gossip and lies are an everyday way of life for many people, but I never got used to their behavior. We tried to stay focused on the bigger picture.

The news about Tsunami-dog was also disturbing. Ever since I had cleaned her up, every male dog in the village wanted a piece of her. She had gotten pregnant shortly before I left, and the puppies had been born while I was away. So as soon as I got back from New York, I raced over to the caretakers' house to find her and her babies. At first I thought she didn't recognize me, because she didn't move when I entered the room and called her name. But then she gave me a few sniffs and our love was rekindled. I was furious to see that she was exhausted and undernourished. It looked like the family hadn't been feeding her. In the corner sat her eight puppies, crammed into a small, cruel cage. At least the puppies resembled the junkyard dog that had followed her everywhere. It put me at ease knowing that her boyfriend would help defend her and her babies in the coming months.

Once Oscar and I had settled in, we saw that many of the NGOs had left, and the aid trucks had stopped coming. Monsoon rains had started, so tourism was nonexistent and the economy was suffering. It was a ghost town. Oscar and I were now the only volunteers left in Peraliya, with very few people working in town and other villages along the coast. An insecure feeling lingered in the air. The neediness in the village had escalated and sad letters asking for money jumped into my hands daily. Some people had begun begging near the train station. In addition, the dangers of the area were becoming more visible, as local tribes had gone back to fighting one another.

On the other hand, there were some bright points of light. Dr. Stein had started breaking ground on the new medical center, and I was thrilled with the thought of the villagers receiving free healthcare. Sebastian, one of our early volunteers, was still working as a doctor down the coast doing great work. In his spare time, he started to operate on the sick and dying animals all around him. And CTEC, where I planned to focus my attention now that I was back, was coming along very well.

Upon my arrival at the tsunami center, the CTEC officers lined up in full uniform against the wall, saluting me as I walked past. I noticed that the walls were now filled with world maps, and books about earthquakes lay on the tabletops. Dr. Novil, my co-founder, told me that he had been busy teaching the new tsunami officers about disaster preparedness and had also been learning about it himself. They practiced evacuation drills daily. They had erected signs along the roads marking safe exit routes leading to higher ground, and warning people about dead-end streets. The CTEC officers made these road signs by hand, spending hundreds of hours creating them. In addition, they made flyers with information about the tsunami center and distributed them to all the villagers in the region.

On that first day back, we had to stop our meeting twice when false tsunami scares sent villagers fleeing into the jungle. At first I thought these were drills the officers had organized to show me their skills, but in fact they were real tsunami scares. The CTEC officers dutifully checked their computers, then made their rounds through the villages, reassuring everyone that it had been a false alarm and that they could stay in their homes. Watching the team in action made me so proud. I thanked Dr. Novil and the officers for their hard work. Later that week, Telstra donated ten new cellphones to our cause.

Word about CTEC was spreading all over Sri Lanka. The police, the Navy, and other members of the military would stop by regularly to check on false tsunami reports. Shortly after the Nicobar earthquake, CTEC received letters from the United Nations officially endorsing the center and one from the minister of social services thanking them on behalf of the Sri Lankan government.

These were strange times in Sri Lanka, ones that made us shake our heads in confusion. So many amazing things were happening, but there were also so many deceptive schemes at work. I was learning that the aid business was a dirty one. I saw how the NGOs and villagers were each trying to take advantage of the other. One of our doctors summed it up especially well: He said that it was more honorable to be an arms dealer than to be in the aid business. The arms dealer says, "I have a gun, do you want to buy it?" He has no hidden agenda. Aid groups, on the other hand, would sometimes misuse and redirect funds in ways that made my blood boil, all in the name of helping people.

The corruption hadn't started with this latest tsunami; it had been going on for decades. But it was magnified by the disaster. I saw villagers begging for new boats, and then turning around and selling them for cash as soon as the aid group had left. Then, a month later, they would beg the next aid group to buy them a boat. Some families received six boats and four houses in that way. Aid groups usually stayed for only two to three weeks before a new team came in to take their place. The new people wouldn't know the villagers and would innocently go forward to help them. As a result, the cunning were getting richer while the honest folks were still waiting for aid. The ones who spoke English received more aid than those who spoke only Sinhalese. Our job was to weed through the lies to find the truths, but it was becoming harder every day.

On the other side of the fence, the NGOs were highly accountable to their donors. In a rush to fulfill that need, some took photos of projects that weren't their own, including ours. I visited websites where NGOs declared that they had rebuilt 2,000 homes when in reality none had been started. One group even had the nerve to post a photo of our hospital on their website. You can imagine my shock when I found it. While NGOs got mired in swamps of paperwork, people truly suffered and millions of tsunami aid dollars sat around in bank accounts and got redirected to other causes. That, in my mind, was the worst crime of all. Of course, there were also some NGOs doing great work, as well as many smaller volunteer groups that offered tremendous help.

CHAPTER 11

For the past thirty years, the Sri Lankan government had been involved in an ugly civil war against the Tamil Tiger rebels. When the tsunami hit, some of the worst damage was in the northern region of the country, which was the stronghold of the Tamil Army. Thankfully, this brought about a cease-fire in order to get aid into the region. But the peace rapidly dissolved into mistrust, and as the months passed, suicide bombings and attacks were on the rise again.

Oscar had returned to training his soccer team, which gave him the idea of holding a soccer match against a Tamil team in Jaffna, on the front lines of the war zone. It was a fantastic and outrageous idea, like getting an Israeli team to play soccer against Hamas in Gaza. I was all for it.

We started out by visiting the heads of the Sri Lankan Soccer Federation and FIFA, the international soccer governing association, in Colombo to get the go-ahead for the match. The officials looked at Oscar as if he had two heads when he proposed his idea, but he kept insisting, and they gave their consent. Oscar then visited the players' homes to gain permission from their parents to come on the trip. He lined up everything on our end.

But two major obstacles still lay ahead, and they required us to fly up to the front lines of the war zone. First, we had to get the support of the Sri Lankan military commanders in the region. Second, we had to meet with Tamil Tiger leaders to ask if we could play a match against them on their territory.

We flew into the Sri Lankan Air Force base in Jaffna. An Army captain we had known from Galle who was now stationed there picked us up. We jumped into his jeep filled with snipers carrying submachine guns and drove through deserted war zones to an Army base. There, a Sri Lankan Army general met with us to discuss the soccer match. The general was excited about the game's potential to build goodwill, but he wanted us to hold the game on the Army base. He thought it would be too dangerous for us to play on Tamil territory, as anyone in the crowd could start throwing grenades at any moment.

Oscar agreed to have his Galle team play one soccer match against the Army team on the Army base there in Jaffna. However, he insisted that his team also be permitted to play a game against the Tamil team on Tamil terroritory, presuming we could get the okay from the Tamil leaders. After a great deal of discussion, the general reluctantly conceded to Oscar's plan. However, he made it clear that his men would not be responsible for our safety when we crossed enemy lines.

With that approval out of the way, we went to meet the Tamil Tiger terrorists to arrange the game against their team. The Army escorted us to a hotel in Jaffna, where we hung around for hours waiting for some sort of contact. Finally, a group of official-looking men in white shirts and ties showed up. We sat drinking tea and discussing the game. They spoke with one another and made phone calls, clearly assessing us all the while.

Then, in a quick turn of events, the men urged us to follow them to their van and we obeyed. Looking back, we were extremely foolish to go with them. It was the equivalent of an unplanned meeting with al-Qaeda. But we had no agenda other than to play soccer, so we felt no fear.

We traveled a long way with the Tamils, passing through many Sri Lankan Army checkpoints. At each stop, the van was thoroughly searched. I observed that some of the men who were traveling with us had missing arms or legs and bullet scars on exposed body parts. Eventually we came to a Tamil Tiger checkpoint. After the van had been searched once more, the driver pulled up to the back of a house. The men instructed us to leave our bags in the vehicle and follow them. Men with Uzi submachine guns surrounded us as we walked out into the middle of a green field to a large, shady tree. Under the tree sat two nicely dressed, athletic men with 9mm guns tied around their waists, surrounded by men with even larger guns.

The well-dressed gentlemen invited us to sit down, and the soccer discussions began again. The Tamil Tigers' main concern was that the Sri Lankan Army should stay away. After three hours of discussion, we agreed to trust the Tamil leaders' word that they wouldn't interfere with the game or with our players if we arrived for the match unprotected. We rose and shook firm hands, and the van raced us back to Jaffna before nightfall.

We visited the Sri Lankan Army general the next day and told him the news: Our Galle team would play a match in Tamil territory against a Tamil team with no Army presence. The general agreed to stay away, but hinted that he would have an undercover unit hiding somewhere nearby just in case anything went wrong. Oscar and I were ecstatic. We couldn't wait for the games to begin, but first we still had quite a bit of work to do and funds to raise.

Plans for the historic soccer matches, which we had decided to call Football Without Boundaries, came together when we received much-needed funding from Mr. Kiha Pimental of Hawaii via our friend Doug Kennedy. Then, a week before our big event was scheduled to take place, the Sri Lankan foreign minister was assassinated in his own home. The government declared a state of emergency and the country came to a standstill. Naturally, they blamed the Tamil Tigers for the incident. We nervously awaited news, wondering if our game would be canceled. I told Oscar not to be intimidated by the assassination. I felt strongly that if we didn't go on with our lives and activities, the terrorists would win.

On August 22, 2005, eight months after the tsunami struck Sri Lanka, Oscar, James, and I sat on a bus with a team of excited Peraliya soccer players who were singing their lungs out. The Sri Lankan military had given us the go-ahead for the soccer tournament. I was the only female in our group. We had brought Dr. Novil along as the team doctor, and the two of us discussed emergency procedures just in case we found ourselves in the middle of a bloody massacre. An older American volunteer named Buddy had joined to help me shoot some footage of the games, as Sunil had been too sick to join us (or so he said—perhaps he felt it was too risky to come). James, the British journalist volunteer who had helped us in the early days, still flew in and out of Sri

Lanka often. He came in from London specially to watch the match and donate jerseys from the Leeds United soccer team.

When we arrived at the gate of the Sri Lankan Air Force base in Galle, where we were to load the plane for Jaffna, the singing stopped. A hush fell over the bus and tensions rose as the players confronted the serious side of this expedition. The airplane ride to Jaffna was tense. When we landed at the Air Force base, Army guards with Uzi submachine guns whisked us onto a bus and drove us through deserted towns and overgrown vegetation to a small hotel for a short rest.

Our first game was against the Tamil team on Tamil territory. We rode a bus out to their stadium without any military protection, unloaded quietly, and nervously approached the arena. There we saw thousands of bicycles parked outside, as well as one United Nations peacekeeping jeep. The huge Tamil players

The Sri Lankan and Tamil Tiger soccer teams shaking hands before the game

formed a line outside the stadium to welcome us. For the first time in thirty years, the two enemies shook hands. Many of the players had had family members killed by relatives of the opposing team. They sized one another up, then the Tamils ushered us into a small changing room where the players could prepare themselves for a different sort of war.

When our little homegrown soccer team walked out onto the field ready to play, there were 4,000 men standing around waiting for the game, which was now behind schedule. The Tamil mayor and the head of the Jaffna Soccer Federation made welcome speeches and placed beautiful flowers around Oscar's neck. The referee came out onto the field and I noticed that he was one of the Tamil Tiger terrorists from the negotiations the week before. He was as strong as a bull and quite a good-looking, rugged man. I found myself blushing as we met eye to eye. I had a thing for warriors. But one point was clear: We wouldn't be arguing with his calls.

The players did a brief warm-up and then it was game on. The Tamil players were taller and a lot older than our players, but they were all good fighting machines. The crowd watched quietly, careful not to betray which side they were rooting for just in case the secret police were nearby. Oscar ran up and down the sidelines screaming his head off like a crazy Sicilian soccer coach. James sat in a chair on the sidelines playing the English commentator. "They are too bloody good!" he yelled out in a stiff British accent. Dr. Novil attended to a player who had just passed out.

I scanned the crowd for potential trouble and saw that Buddy had gone missing. He had offered to shoot the game on my little video camera, assuring me that he had been the video guy at his church. What I didn't know was that Buddy was a heavy drinker and had started boozing at breakfast. By now he was toast. I found him passed out under a tree, his mind dancing with mermaids, and I took over filming the game myself. Later, when we looked at his footage, we saw a lot of images of ground and sky.

It was a great game and both sides played well, while the civil war was put on hold for ninety minutes. The opposing Tamil team won 3–0, but I'd never been to a sporting event where I had wanted the other team to win more. Not because I didn't think we would get out alive if we won, but simply because they needed it more. The Tamil team showed off their unrepressed excitement by screaming chants and holding the huge silver trophy Oscar had brought high in the air. Our losing Sinhalese players sat around in disappointment. But back on the bus, Oscar told them he was proud of them and spoke about its being a historic day for Sri Lanka with the two enemies coming together for one common reason.

We held a party for both teams back at our hotel in Jaffna. Oscar gave everyone Football Without Boundaries T-shirts to wear, and the spirit of unity continued on into the night as we all wore matching shirts and celebrated together. The Sinhalese sang traditional songs in their language and the Tamil sang songs back in their language. James, Oscar, and I looked at one another in sheer amazement, relishing the fact that we had pulled off this event without bloodshed. The Tamil terrorists and the Sri Lankan generals had held true to their word and stayed away.

The players started to get drunk, and the Tamil leaders thought it best to quit while we were ahead. As they left, they told us that they had never had a game or celebration like this in their lives. They were giddy with happiness. Now that the special day and night were over, they had to work out a way to sneak back across the borders without being captured. I blushed at the cute Tamil referee as he said good-bye, and watched him walk out of my life.

The next day, we woke up early and traveled by military escort to the large base where we would be playing the Sri Lankan Army team. The whole Army had turned out to watch. Thousands of the corps and engineers stood around the field in the roasting sun, while the commandos, generals, and other high-ranking officials sat under the trees in full uniform and maroon berets. The event was charming and civilized. We ate tiny tea sandwiches served by men wearing white gloves, a ritual left over from the British colonial days. With so many people watching the game, I wondered if anyone was left out there to fight the war.

From the moment the game began, it became apparent that we were the stronger team. By the second half, we were so far ahead that I walked over to Oscar and told him to take it easy so as not to embarrass our hosts. Oscar pulled some of the better players from the field and let the weaker ones have a go. Still, we won the game 5–0.

After the match, we met with more generals, and then were taken to a special holding area. It was a garden with a huge tree in the middle of it. I think they put us there to protect us until our plane left. We drank and ate to our hearts' content and soon the players began break-dancing.

CHAPTER 12

Before Oscar and I had left for New York, my cousin Christine had given Chamilla $1,000 to start a communications center that sold fresh smoothies, which she called the Tsunami Juice Café. She used the money to buy a fax machine, blenders, and outdoor tables and chairs. Oscar and I were pleased to frequent the business when we returned to Peraliya, feeling happy for Chamilla's new lease on life. I was on a tight budget, as always, living off small donations from my family and friends, so I couldn't invest any money in Chamilla's cause. But I always directed new volunteers and visitors to her café, and I'd stop by as often as I could. Instead of paying forty cents for an item, I would leave five dollars on the table. It wasn't much, but it was all I could afford, and I certainly thought Chamilla would see it as a gesture of goodwill.

One day at the Tsunami Juice Café, Chamilla brought me a large, frothing drink and served it up with a cat's meow, as sweet and caring as could be. I took a sip, but the drink tasted disgusting so I poured it out on a plant when she wasn't looking. Later, Chamilla's brother told me that the drink she'd given me had something in it. He said that Chamilla felt my regular, if small, donations were a pathetic act on my part. She believed that I had thousands of dollars in the bank and was refusing to help her. Even so, in a sort of wishful, delusional way, I continued to defend and love her.

When Oscar and I first arrived in Peraliya, we were thrown into the responsibility of running an IDP camp for more than 3,000 people. That took priority in our lives. There was so much devastation and loss around us that it sucked all the love and energy out of me daily. My only quality time with Oscar would be a quick dinner before we passed out at night.

Oscar had also become more and more agitated lately. Relationships can be difficult enough to manage in your hometowns, but take someone you thought you knew thousands of miles away and add a billion more pressures, and you might meet an entirely new person. Oscar had started raising his voice and cursing at me in front of volunteers and villagers, which disturbed me deeply. I understood that he was more prone to outbursts than I was—he was from a Sicilian family that was accustomed to yelling. I had been raised in a quiet atmosphere where people raised their voices only if they were in danger. When I first visited Sicily, I had watched in shock as Oscar's really sweet family argued around the dinner table. I pleaded with them to stop fighting. They looked at me in surprise. They weren't fighting, they explained. This was just the way they communicated.

Nevertheless, Oscar and I enjoyed many beautiful moments in Sri Lanka, sharing brilliant sunsets and swimming with turtles at the beach. We took motocross bike rides into the jungles and led the weekly swimming days with the children. Oscar was passionately committed to our work in Peraliya, and this bonded us together. During our time there, a deeper friendship developed between us, one based on respect for what we were achieving each day. But while we had long discussions about how to improve the village, we never spoke about the tensions between us. Whenever we went far away from the village, he seemed to relax and the old, fun Oscar would return. But once we were within a twenty-mile radius of Peraliya, his negative emotions would swell again.

Now that we were the only two volunteers left in Peraliya village, we were spread especially thin, between running CTEC and the rebuilding activities. Oscar was operating at full speed, trying hard to right a hundred wrongs, but things weren't right between us. We harbored a quiet anger toward each other. But then again, we understood that we only had each other.

One day in late August, I received an urgent phone call from Oscar saying that he had been hurt in a motorbike accident. He pleaded for me to come quickly, telling me that he was on the main street of Hikkaduwa. My heart throbbed like a jackhammer as I raced on my scooter to help him. My bike had a top speed of sixty miles per hour. I spoke to it like a racehorse, telling it to hurry up. I almost fell off a few times as I charged along the highway, overtaking everything in my way.

The Hikkaduwa main road was busy and long, so I raced right past Oscar without seeing him. When I couldn't find him, I doubled back. I did this a few times before I finally spotted him outside a medical clinic getting help. I thanked God he was alive and rushed over to examine his hurt leg. He said that the bus had pushed him into another motorbike coming toward him, and that both drivers had been thrown off their bikes. Oscar was very lucky to be alive; usually an accident with a bus in Sri Lanka meant death. As he finished telling me his story, I became faint and nearly passed out. I sat down on the ground in shock. I had been dealing with everyone else's deaths for months, but this had happened to the person closest to me.

We took a van to a hospital in Galle to get an X ray of Oscar's leg. Upon arriving there, I noticed a clothesline where washed latex gloves hung out to dry for reuse later. Not a good sign. Inside, we recognized many of the doctors and nurses who had come to help us at the Peraliya field hospital and they were very friendly to us. Oscar's foot and leg had three fractures and he had open wounds going deep down to the bone, which would have to heal before the plaster could be put on his broken foot.

In Sri Lanka, there were always two prices for everything, from a visit to a national park, to hotel accommodations, to food in restaurants: Sri Lankan price and tourist price. We were used to paying the local price with our Sri Lankan friends in our village, but when we were alone on the road, we were always overcharged like tourists. The local hospital bill came to 220 rupees, equivalent to about twenty-two dollars U.S., and the officials should have charged us that price since they knew us and were familiar with our work in Peraliya. Instead they charged us the full tourist price, which added up to a few hundred dollars that we didn't have.

A week before the accident, Oscar and I had moved from Hikkaduwa to a jungle house inland. We wanted to be in a quieter area away from the villagers who turned up at our guesthouse daily to beg for money. It was a classic Sri Lankan home and had a beautiful garden full of exotic fruits and flowers with a little Buddha shrine in the middle of it.

I brought Oscar back to the jungle house to recuperate after his accident. He wasn't a happy patient, completely helpless and confined to a couch. He couldn't get up on his own or even hop around, as it would pull on his stitches and they would start to bleed. Thankfully Sunil offered to help me out. The two of us would have to carry Oscar in his full weight to the toilet and to bed. When Sunil wasn't around, I had to lift him on my own. He was an extremely heavy patient and it made my back ache. What's more, I was now completely alone in the village. I was torn between three worlds: running the tsunami center, opening businesses, and racing back and forth to care for Oscar. I tried to keep him satisfied, but there was no consoling him, and his words to me now were always harsh and full of pain. I had been in war zones, famines, earthquakes, floods, and poverty-torn countries and had been charged by hippos and lions in Africa, but looking after Oscar turned out to be the most trying experience of all.

The village monk and a few young local boys would visit Oscar regularly. They'd sit around and play Karum, a local Sri Lankan board game in which players flick a round, flat disk across the board by placing their finger on it. Sunil and his girlfriend, Juliet, would also come over at night to play Karum with Oscar until very late. Our landlord, who lived in the house in front of us, was suspicious of anyone staying with us after midnight. He thought they were living there and cheating him by not paying the rent. The accusation was far from the truth. But one night when Juliet had lain down on the couch to rest, the landlord burst into the house and threw her and Sunil out. A fuming Oscar called the police, who took the landlord away for interrogations. We found another house to rent a quarter of a mile inland.

The villagers were trying to get back to their everyday lives, which also meant that gang activity was in full swing. Suddenly our village wasn't the innocent place we had stumbled across after the tsunami. It was full of murderers, thieves, and very desperate people. The first murder of thirteen that we were to experience took place at the school, where a group of teenagers were playing cricket. The leader of a gang from the village next door walked up to one of the boys, held a gun to his head, and then shot him in the head, heart, and throat. He and his gang stood there watching the boy die. Apparently, the teenager had had words with him earlier that morning and this was the gang leader's revenge. Sadly, villagers often settled disputes that way. The murder cases were left for the police to solve, but doing so was a lost cause: Nobody would come forward as a witness, as they feared that they, too, would be murdered.

People warned us to stay out of these local problems or our work would be jeopardized. As it was, in every direction, villagers were begging me for money, so I found myself staying away from Peraliya altogether and working longer and longer hours in the peaceful sanctuary of the tsunami center.

In late August, New Orleans was hit by Hurricane Katrina and it rocked the aid workers in Sri Lanka, especially the Americans. We felt hopeless being so far away, but we also felt that we had to finish what we had started. Many aid organizations pulled out of Sri Lanka to go help in New Orleans, but we couldn't turn our backs on the villagers.

Oscar, his broken foot, and I loved our new house, which was surrounded by a beautiful garden. Since it was the monsoon season, we acquired it for a very cheap price, around the same rate as our old guesthouse at the beach. It had a ground floor where Oscar could sleep and also get out to the couch area to sit during the day. In the afternoons, monkeys swung in to eat the mangoes they had picked from the trees above us. We watched them dancing around the trees and coaxed them closer with bananas.

One day while I was working in a neighboring village, attending to a lady having a heart attack, Oscar kept calling on my cellphone demanding that I bring him food. He screamed at me through the phone while I balanced the poor lady on my arm. Then I nearly dropped her. I threw my phone on the ground in order to catch her with both arms and lay her on the ground. I attended to her for a few panicked hours and then finally made it home with some food from a local shop. By that time, Oscar was irate. He wouldn't listen to a word about what I had been through. His curses struck the air around me like lightning striking an electrical tower. I felt numb.

Oscar was making me miserable but I couldn't walk away from him like this. He was crippled in a strange land that I was responsible for bringing him to, and I was the only one there to care for him. When my husband had abandoned me after my accident many years before, I had sworn that I would never do the same thing to anyone else. So I pushed on in silence and tears as Oscar's demands grew more outrageous, reaching deeper and deeper inside myself for strength.

Whenever I needed a time-out, I'd go to Doadandoa, my secret Sri Lankan island. I could walk out to it only at low tide, when the rushing water would swarm around my thighs. The journey was tricky to maneuver. The ocean floor had a jagged coral bottom with invisible holes in it that swallowed me when I lost my footing. But once I made it there, I was in paradise. I would stand on the large rocks to feel the ocean's spray smacking me in the face.

Friendly fisherman waved to me as they headed out to sea. On the island grew large coconut trees, and hundreds of black birds circled overhead.

It was this secret Sri Lankan island where I went to be alone with my thoughts. I listened to the silence, and it was loud. I listened to the birds and the wind and the ocean and the crickets and the boats and the fish and the rain. I listened to the grass growing and the ants walking and the butterflies eating and the shells breathing. I heard the sun singing and the sky laughing and I heard my creator as I listened to myself. The world is full of beautiful silences if we only listen. I lay under the swaying palms like a stranded mermaid waiting to be rescued, but nobody ever came.

When Oscar's open wounds healed, I took him to the hospital to have the doctor set his broken foot. The cast had been on for three swelteringly hot days when a nasty infection developed between his toes. It was so hot in Sri Lanka that even the smallest mosquito bite turned into a festering wound within days. I had to treat him every few hours. After a few days, Oscar couldn't bear it anymore. He took out his switchblade and started hacking the plaster off his foot to free his toes. It was the way he hacked at his foot that disturbed me—one false strike would have sent the knife straight through his leg. He chopped at it for hours until his foot was free. I knew then that things had to change or I would risk losing my sanity.

I had been unsuccessful in my search for a wheelchair for Oscar. Then, out of the blue, someone gave me a quiet lead that a certain president of a Lion's Club in the area might have access to one. However, he wanted to meet us first to assess us. We drove to his home along unfamiliar roads and down back alleys until we came to a sliding fence where guards brought us inside to meet him. We sipped Ceylon tea and made small talk. I felt as though I were participating in some type of espionage. The other men sitting around us whispered, and then the president indicated that they would be in contact with us when they had located their target.

A few days later, we got the call: A wheelchair was being made available to us. We couldn't believe our luck. Now Oscar would be able to get around the house independently. Months later we found out, much to our sadness, that the Lion's Club men had taken the wheelchair away from a crippled boy. Had we had any clue at the time, we never would have accepted it. Life could be harsh in Sri Lanka.

On the night of September 5, the monsoon rains and wind surged through the village, cutting off all the power in the area. I received a call from CTEC, which was running on backup generators: A fire was raging. A can of petrol had been knocked over in one of the temporary homes and exploded into flames. CTEC called the fire department and rushed to the scene with their megaphones to help get people to safety, arriving before any of the official agencies. Dr. Novil was managing the medical care.

I grabbed my flashlight and put on my cargo pants, stuffing its pockets with medical supplies. Sunil and I were running out the door when Oscar declared that he was coming with us. I didn't know what kind of help he thought he was going to be. I argued that I couldn't take an injured person in a wheelchair into an emergency situation and demanded that he stay home.

Sunil and I raced over to the village. The fire had already en-

gulfed thirty homes, but thanks in large part to the efforts of the
CTEC officers, the flames were subsiding. Eighty-four people had
lost everything—again. Villagers walked around in despair asking why they were being punished so much. This time I began to
question it all myself. I held a woman tightly as she sobbed in my
arms. I was rummaging through the charcoal rubble when I recognized a charred Disney doll I had given to a family upon my arrival in Sri Lanka. It felt like hope had abandoned this place.

Then I looked over to the road, where I spied a tuk-tuk with a
wheelchair hanging off the back. It was Oscar; he had come to
the village on his own to help. He maneuvered his chair over
rough ground and comforted people. Oscar was lucky this time.
Coming into a dangerous situation like that in a wheelchair
could have cost us both our lives.

Luckily, no lives were lost in the fire. There was one strange in-
jury that night, however: A man was bitten by a snake. I had felt
the evil presence of the snake when I arrived back in Sri Lanka
from New York, and I was prepared to do battle. One of the volunteers later told me that he had left his bike on the ground
when he rushed over to help, and it had been stolen. The snake
was alive again, and worse things were in store.

Driving to the village on my scooter, I felt exhausted. It was the
third morning in a row that I had burst into tears for no real reason. Oscar was driving me crazy at home. When I arrived in Peraliya, the women were already complaining and the men
appeared drunker than usual. The village had flooded again due
to rising sea levels, and I had just run out of Chanel No. 5.

The chief came by and suggested that I help a woman he knew
who needed assistance. When I told him that I had already

helped her, he didn't believe me and dragged her over for a confrontation. When he asked her to tell him the truth about whether or not she had received help from us, she lied and denied it. I stood there feeling as though I had been stung by bees. I distinctly remembered the goods and services I had given her, including treating her wounds when she was close to death from infection. I asked her to look me in the eyes as she repeated her answer. When she again denied the help, I felt my heart physically crack. However, I remained quiet, knowing that if I proved her to be a liar, she would lose face in front of the village chief and be run out of Peraliya. I couldn't wish that fate on anyone.

I pulled myself together and got to work. But later that same day, when we were working in the schoolyard, a village lady came by screaming and pointing her fingers at Sunil and Chamilla. I knew her to be a tribal ringleader. She breathed fire at our interpreters, accusing them of being the cause of all the villagers' troubles by not accurately translating what they were saying to us. Kumara, a regular troublemaker, stormed over in mid-argument. He yelled at Chamilla and the ringleader, telling them they should both be beaten for the things they were saying. He accused them of accepting money from the foreigners and then denying it behind their backs. The village chief joined the fray with his Communist theories. It sounded like an orchestra of seagulls.

I sat in a nearby chair, slumped over in front of all the arguing people, and wept openly. I felt that I'd had enough and wanted to go home. I wanted my bubble bath and sushi at Nobu. At the same time, I also knew that if we left now, no one would help the villagers, and I couldn't bear that thought, no matter how tough things had been lately.

But the snake reared its head once more. My favorite pet,

Tsunami-dog, was always at my side, and I knew that some of the villagers were jealous of the attention I gave her. A few angry drunken men made our lives hell by throwing stones at her and kicking her when she was alone. Then one day she went missing, and I walked the entire village asking if anyone had seen her. A kind villager led me to her, lying on his family bed. She whimpered like a baby and I held her in my arms as if she were my child. The villager told me that a drunken man had broken all her legs just for the fun of it. I was speechless. It was as if my own legs had been broken. I lay hugging my Tsunami-dog, my heart shredded into a trillion pieces. It was a good thing for the man who had hurt her that I couldn't find him, because I wanted to tie him to a tree and have a thousand dogs pee on him.

I lost my innocent faith in humankind that day when I saw just how cruel, jealous, and evil people could be to one another. I was inconsolable. I missed Donny and Bruce and I missed my mum, who would usually give me a hug and tell me everything was going to be fine. But I was a big girl now and I had to look after myself.

Sunil had been taking small jobs in film with NGOs to pay for his room and board. But these days, he dedicated most of his time to helping Nuwan, the little boy who had been disabled when he fell into the pit of burning oil, learn to walk again. Since Nuwan's father was blind and his mother was mentally challenged, Sunil realized that if he didn't teach Nuwan to walk again, no one would.

Helping meant that Sunil had to bicycle to Nuwan's village three times a day, four miles round-trip each time, to make sure the boy got food and stretched his legs. To make matters worse,

Sunil had acquired many enemies—villagers who thought he was making millions of dollars from his filming, when in reality he earned very little. Tribal gangs would wait for him to pass by and then throw stones at him, but they never deterred him. Sunil got medical help for Nuwan from volunteers and small charities. He often had to forcefully convince Nuwan's father to do the rehabilitation exercises with his son. Sunil also spent long, agonizing hours at an Ayurvedic clinic, where doctors rubbed natural local oils into Nuwan's body and engaged in painful forced manipulation of his legs. The burden lay heavy on Sunil, who often went days without food so that Nuwan could have medicine and sustenance.

Being a cameraman was an important job; documenting images of our work in Peraliya would help us spread the word and bring further assistance back to the area. But Sunil went beyond the call of duty when he decided to help Nuwan walk again. Sunil's example proved to me that although we all may define ourselves by our jobs or the subjects we studied at school, we actually have hundreds of skills at our disposal and can do many things to help.

Toward the end of a long healing road, Sunil put Nuwan on a bicycle and pushed it fast along the road. Then Sunil let go. I am certain he will never forget that moment in his life. There could be only two outcomes: Nuwan would either freeze and fall off the bike, further injuring himself, or he would start to use his legs to pedal and stay on the bike. He chose to pedal. The sight of Nuwan the crippled boy using his legs for the first time since his accident, a huge grin covering his face, must have had all the angels in the kingdom smiling.

———

We had celebrated *Poya,* the monthly ceremony for the full moon, before. In September, however, *Poya* was called the *Perahera* festival. It was a special celebration that drew tens of thousands of people to the coastline. Holidays up to that point had been quiet and low-key, but this was a different story. The festival organizers approached CTEC to set up a computer at the temple to keep worried villagers abreast of any possible tsunamis. It would only take one person yelling "Tsunami!" to cause a stampede that could lead to many deaths. Only the week before, in Iran, someone at a mosque had yelled "Suicide bomber!" and more than 500 people had been injured and several killed during the stampede.

CTEC set up a booth with computers in the heart of the festival and decorated it in CTEC banners. The officers wore their new uniforms and handed out flyers advertising the center. It was a brilliant day with the coast exploding into color and dance. Stunning oranges and reds flashed past a turquoise sea as babies and grandparents celebrated life and death. Change was in the air. The devastated region was transformed by dancing elephants, acrobats, maidens, and conquering pirates. Hot sweet curries and spicy roti sizzled by the road. Everyone appreciated CTEC being there to protect them, and policemen kept coming over to hug me.

A few hours before the festival, a reported 5.8-magnitude earthquake struck in nearby Myanmar, which set off a tsunami scare and sent villagers heading inland. CTEC sprang into action, quickly restoring order using their speaker systems and motorbikes. The festivities continued on through the night, with firewalking on the beach. I hung out with many of the villagers, holding hands, laughing, and dancing.

By the end of October, with Oscar at our home in the jungle recovering, I was the only volunteer left in the village and I had
begun to stand out. I would walk faster on my daily home visits,
knowing that dangerous gang members were watching my every
move. A gang from a neighboring village had killed a mentally
unstable villager whom we had grown to love. They had chopped
out his eyes, nose, ears, and mouth, cutting his body into hundreds of pieces. It wasn't safe for a white woman to be in the village after dark. I wasn't scared, because I had nothing left to give
them but love, but I wasn't going to be stupid, either.

After I sat on the chief's roof one night gazing at another liq-
uid sunset, he rode with me on my scooter out to the main road
to make sure that I was safe. It was a ravishing night. I watched
the palm trees swaying as I passed the new turtle hatchery. I
thought about all the volunteers who had helped us, and I was
filled with love for them. People from every nation had rebuilt
the village together. They had come eager to help and left with
sunburn, dehydration, and memories to last a lifetime.

The continuous gossip was trying—tales of us running away
with millions of dollars in tsunami aid money. These stories
grew old. We took comfort in the fact that those who really knew
us knew the truth.

I continued to devote most of my time to developing the
tsunami center with Dr. Novil. Meanwhile, Oscar worked on
plans for the rebuilding of the new Peraliya School with the
money our friend Kym had raised for that purpose in Canada.

Kym had entrusted the money to an NGO called Free the Children so we wouldn't have to worry about building matters and accountability.

We had wanted to get started with the school right away, but unfortunately over the months the project had come across many roadblocks. The Italian government had acquired the Sri Lankan contract to rebuild twenty-three schools along the coast, including the one in Peraliya. Oscar had attended endless meetings with the Board of Education to try to resolve the matter, but bureaucracy had won in the end. After failing to convince the Italians to hand over that one school contract, Oscar and representatives from Free the Children scouted in the Tamil areas to the north, which had been devastated by both the tsunami and the civil war. They came up with a new plan to build a school in the Ampara district of northeast Sri Lanka, where it was desperately needed. The children there were among the poorest in the country. We felt it was meant to be.

Our villagers, on the other hand, didn't see it that way. All they understood was that the rebuilding of the Peraliya School hadn't started yet. They wondered where all the money had gone. Explaining to our villagers that we were building the school in a village to the north because they were going to get one anyway didn't go down too well. No amount of translation could explain the situation to them in a satisfactory manner. They felt that we had betrayed them. If only they knew how hard we had tried to make things go their way.

In December, wonderful Christmas gifts arrived: Bruce, Donny, Sebastian, Stefan, and James had all decided to return to Sri

Lanka for two weeks over the holidays, and our volunteer gang was reunited. It was thrilling to see them again. We walked around the village and met with a warm reception from the locals. "Hello, machan!" families would call out when they saw Donny. It was so good to see the villagers smiling again and saying, "We love you, we love you." The chief spotted us walking along the train tracks and raced over to hug everyone.

Bruce pointed out that the color was back: beautiful green grass filled with thousands of purple flowers, small palms, and mango, banana, and papaya trees. Living things had sprouted all over the once polluted destruction. We visited our favorite roti shop and invited everyone to join us for lunch.

The days passed and the cheery hellos turned into real needs as villagers slowly pulled us aside to discuss their problems, which usually had to do with money. The purple flowers were fading fast. On closer inspection, the temporary shacks, which were supposed to be inhabited for only six months, were rotting; the salt air had eaten through the tin roofs. The monsoons had arrived late and flooding had been heavy. It was time for a restoration project.

Meanwhile, Oscar and I wanted to find out where all the promised tsunami aid money had gone, so we embarked on a mission to the U.N. office in Galle to ask them directly. The U.N. representatives showed us paperwork documenting promised money, but the fact was that most of it hadn't arrived. Many of the early tsunami pledges had been broken completely. Other money was sitting in bank accounts around the world, with people not knowing where to send it. Still other funds were passing through dozens of hands and being whittled away by corruption. It was a mind-boggling maze. Next we visited the Galle mayor, who also revealed that he had no clue where the money was or how to access the bank accounts—and he was in charge of the most destroyed region in the country.

I observed that in the past week, there had been minor bickering between the volunteers. People were here in a different capacity from the early days and felt at a loss as to what to do next, although there was still plenty to do. It would take another twenty years to rebuild from the tsunami, but with fewer emergency-level needs, volunteers had more time on their hands. Many of them felt guilty about going to the beach or taking a swim, though their behavior was perfectly acceptable. The heart of a volunteer wants to go *go go go*, but it is important to look after yourself as well.

The situation was different for Oscar and me. We weren't working in Peraliya anymore and didn't even go into the village that often. Instead, we focused on larger-scale projects, from which many more people could benefit. I was still deep in work mode with CTEC to develop it along the coastline. Oscar was busy getting the school built and developing soccer and sports programs throughout the country. Our plates were more than full and it felt like our work there would never end.

Christmas day was particularly joyful that year. We had so much to be thankful for in our lives. I had brought Christmas decorations from New York and created a special Christmas lunch for the returning volunteers at our monkey house in the jungle. We sat around a long table that we had dragged out into the garden. We reflected on the happier and sadder moments of our adventure. We laughed a lot and felt guilty about eating such a good meal when we knew that many local people were short on food.

Christmas lunch with the volunteers

But we came to the conclusion that we had worked hard and deserved it. The friendships we had formed were strong because of what we had been through together—though we all agreed that back in our own worlds we probably would have never been friends.

The next day, December 26, 2005, would mark the one-year anniversary of the tsunami. The celebration was not quite what we had expected. Our village was shut out of its own memorial. Later I wrote in my journal: *"Today they institutionalized the one-year anniversary of the tsunami. After they left, the real ceremonies began."*

The government and the Army took over the ceremonies and excluded the local villagers along with the village monks, the chief, and all the volunteers. Also not invited was our friend, the godfather to Peraliya village, the Honorable Sri Lankan Trade and

Commerce Minister Jerarj Fernandoupulle. I knew President Mahinda had no clue of his administration's blunders, but I wasn't happy about it. The government pageant involved a procession of expensive NGO jeeps, most of which we had never seen near the village. We tried to get into the reception area but they blocked access, claiming they were nervous about possible suicide bombers. Security was tight. The military lined the streets with machine guns and tanks, and collected cellphones for storage.

I turned away from the swollen crowds and walked down to the beach to join the children frolicking in the water. The monsoon swells were long gone, replaced by an intoxicating sea lapping the white shore. The children were giggling around the waves. I watched them trust the sea again. They had come a long way. For the first time, I thought to myself, "They're going to be okay." Across the road, pompous speeches clogged the air. Then President Mahinda followed with a beautiful, well-thought-out speech, which I could just barely hear above the sound of the crashing waves.

By the late afternoon, the government officials had left, and the villagers and volunteers headed to the beach for a private ceremony. The village women had written letters to their dead. They lined the beach with candles, bowing before them to pray and set the letters alight. It was a quiet sunset full of reflections followed by a soft night of reminiscing. I was with my new family and my mind was calm.

We planned New Year's dinner on the beach and hired a local guesthouse to cook for us. It was a beautiful scene right out of the movie *The Blue Lagoon,* with a fire nearby and candles and ferns spread over the table. Donny was there with his seventeen-year-old daughter, whom he had brought back with him on this trip. He had proudly showed her around the village, sharing his adventures. Volunteers glowed with healthy tans. Some played their guitars around the fire. At midnight, the locals set off fireworks, which exploded in ribbons over the sea. We held one another in love and made toasts to 2006. I felt alive and beautiful and I wanted everyone in the world to feel that way. This was a happiness that no one could ever take away from me.

Over the next couple of weeks, many of the volunteers and NGOs left. Oscar and I were alone again. The tsunami recovery effort was going to take decades, but there weren't many people left to help.

Oscar and I made plans in mid-January to drive up to the Ampara district to visit the new school being built with Kym's fund-raising money. It would be a two-day journey into the Tamil-occupied war zone. Tori, our Muslim Tamil van driver from our first weeks in Sri Lanka, agreed to drive us. Oscar's Italian friend Marco, who had flown in to film with us, also came along.

First, we stopped to visit President Mahinda in the capital. Oscar, Marco, and I waited at the president's headquarters for many hours, but as we had arrived unannounced and many people were lined up to see him, we abandoned that mission. We left word that we were in town and booked a room at the Nippon hotel. Major Shanaka, the head of the president's security forces, came to visit us there for a drink and we discussed the dangers of the journey ahead. He also made a call to a commando camp in the north where we could stay on the first part of our journey. We set off the next day.

We arrived at the camp at night and were immediately surrounded by military men with submachine guns. The commandos were quite hospitable. They gave us an officer's house to stay in and the head of the camp, Major Janaka, joined us for dinner. I was thrilled to be there. I brought up the possibility of coming back to train with the commandos at a later date. He wholeheartedly agreed but I think he may have been humoring me, even though I was dead serious. The major marked our maps with alternative roads we could take, which the Army had cleared and therefore shouldn't have land mines on them. I noted that he had said "shouldn't have," which didn't sound very reassuring.

As we slept, we heard muffled explosions in far-off places. We rose early to get a start on the day, heading cautiously into the unknown. We passed fields of women working the crops and they waved to us as we drove by in our van. When we stopped to say hello, they giggled shyly and asked for lipstick. I handed over my MAC spice-colored lip liner to great bursts of joy, and they ran back into the fields. My newly acquired skill of speaking the Sinhalese language was of no use to me now; everyone here spoke Tamil. We drove past Hindu temples, Buddhist shrines, and Islamic mosques. In this region, I came across the most beautiful shade of green. I called it "paddy field green." It was unlike any color I had seen before. I sat glued to the van window taking many blurred photos.

We passed through numerous checkpoints where military men nervously approached our van for inspection. They didn't look happy. We guessed they had probably been sitting at these posts away from their families for years. I asked them if the roads were safe and they gave us small grins as if to say, "Are they ever?" We traveled all day along the tsunami-ravaged coastline where clearly no one had come to help. At one point, we came to a jagged one-lane road covered in four feet of water. We let a few cars pass us and then carefully drove through the rushing river by following the same route they had chosen. We realized that these large holes must have been created by exploding land mines.

After crossing many more military checkpoints, we finally arrived in the Ampara district in the late afternoon, just as we had finished listening to Pink Floyd's entire collection. There weren't many bicycles and there were noticeably fewer cars; everyone got around on foot. We were eager to find somewhere to stay before dark, so we drove to the beach area, which was the tourist part of town. It was deserted. Many of the hotels were boarded up due to tsunami damage.

We stopped at a small guesthouse that looked functional, and Oscar and Marco walked around to find the owner while I raced over to the beach to play with some stray dogs. To our relief, the place was operational. The owner brought us drinks as we lay in hammocks watching the sun melt into the sea. He led us to tiny rooms that had hole-riddled mosquito nets and dirty sheets covering the beds. In the back, there was a tiny shower where a few drops of cold water leaked out and cockroaches crawled around the walls.

It was tranquil and eerily quiet as we walked along the beach-front looking for signs of life and somewhere to eat. We found only one place open, where a small group of local men were playing cards. We were the only foreigners around. The meal was slow in coming, so I walked over to the beach to look at the boats. While I was there, I befriended a dog who followed me along the shore. He moved closer to me, letting out a peculiar bark I hadn't heard from a dog before. The strange howling grew louder and the dog moved even closer. I forgot all about my "dog whisperer" gifts and became scared. I screamed out for Oscar and the dog leaped at me, knocking me down. It wasn't friendly play; this dog wanted to mate with me and had become excited by my touch. He wanted to show me his dominance. He started nipping at my legs, and just then Oscar came to my rescue. He pulled the dog off me and frightened him away. I was thoroughly shaken.

We arrived back at our guesthouse to an urgent text from Major Shanaka, with whom we had just met in Colombo, telling us there was going to be a terrorist attack somewhere in our area tonight. He was very concerned for our safety. He wanted to send the military in to help get us out. We didn't even consider his offer. If we had learned one thing about this war, it was that the military were the biggest targets of all, and we were safer being away from them. The Tamil Tigers didn't target foreigners. Major Shanaka then sent a flurry of anxious texts warning us that we should leave the area at once.

We glanced around the hotel and down the coast. There was no one in sight; we were all alone. I wondered if others had known about the attacks as well and had fled to their homes. We debated leaving, but by now it was after 10 p.m. and we knew there could be land mines on the roads, so we decided to remain until first light. We were all too aware that land mines didn't discriminate between military men and tourists. I felt a rush of excitement as we discussed our plans. I changed into my cargo pants, grabbed a flashlight and emergency gear, and lay down to sleep with one eye open.

At first light, we packed the car and headed an hour north to find the new school. It was a tense ride. Oscar yelled at me for wearing flip-flops rather than hiking boots, wondering how I was going to run away if confronted by danger. He was right, but the nervous way he snapped at me made me cringe. I was over his bossy attitude. Along the drive, we passed through dirty, poverty-stricken towns and spied commandos walking through the jungle checking the trees. It was obvious they weren't looking for mangoes.

Finally, we made it to the area where they had started building the new school. Oscar held my hand and we took a deep breath, letting out months of struggle and hard work with losing the rights to build the new school at Peraliya. It had been challenging, but our sadness turned to hope as we quickly realized that the new school was meant to be here. We walked through the grounds and tearfully watched a miracle growing around us. In the schoolyard, we met some children and their parents. Tori, our Tamil driver, translated for us as we told them about Kym Anthony, the banker from Canada who had raised the money to build their new school. They were very happy about it. A little girl sang a thank-you song to Kym into the video camera.

After we had inspected the construction efforts and met a few more people, our mission to visit the school was over. Major Shanaka advised that the roads were clear. It was time for us to get out while we still were able. We headed home safely to Hikkaduwa with our hearts full of joy. Back in civilization, we read about the attacks that had occurred the night before. Twelve Navy officers had been blown up in a bus near our guesthouse. We had made the right decision in staying put.

In the coming weeks, we continued our work and waited in frustration for the Italian government to start rebuilding the Peraliya

School, but they were nowhere to be seen. Meanwhile, Kym's Free the Children foundation had already almost finished building the school at Ampara. They also gave us a small amount of money to pay for our continued living expenses in the Hikkaduwa region and return plane tickets to the United States. CTEC was growing and we had developed over eighty community points along the coast—villages where a group of people had taken responsibility for getting tsunami warnings out to their people. CTEC had given them cellphones, radios, and signboards.

With the programs and small businesses we'd put in place up and running, and the rebuilding we had accomplished, it felt like it was time, at last, for Oscar and me to leave for good. Separating myself from Sri Lanka would require a herculean effort, but I knew that I needed to get back to my life in New York.

In February of 2006, fourteen months after the tsunami tragedy, Oscar and I bade a more final farewell to the villagers, the chief, our translators, the CTEC officers, and Tsunami-dog. We returned to New York for good.

CHAPTER 13

Readjusting to life in New York City after over a year of bare-bones existence in the developing world proved more difficult than I had imagined. Volunteers wrote me emails saying that they didn't fit back into their lives anymore, and I could empathize. But I told them that it was a good thing because it would mean more change for the world in the future. I urged them not to forget what they had learned in Sri Lanka. It was also time for me to begin sorting through the tsunami footage.

We had come home with more than three hundred videotapes of our tsunami experiences. When we had first arrived in Pera-liya, we were working very hard, so I pulled out my little video camera for at most ten minutes a day. At first, nobody in the village had a problem with it. Somehow they knew the purpose was to bring further help to the area. It was only much later, when Sunil was shooting all over and for longer hours, that some villagers became suspicious that he was making money off them, although that was far from the truth. We had gone to Sri Lanka to volunteer for two weeks and we could not have known how long we would end up staying or how much footage we would end up shooting. All I did know was that I had a story to tell.

I decided that I wanted to create a documentary film that would encourage people to volunteer and help raise money for CTEC. It would be a road map to volunteering and the message would be that everyone is needed. The problem was that we had no money. Thankfully, our friends Richard Belfiore and Dave Pederson gave thirty minutes of footage to the *Supersize Me* documentary filmmaker Morgan Spurlock for viewing. He called us and said that he wanted to be part of the film. He started out by giving us money to live on while we completed it. Morgan was a sweet, genuine guy with a passion for the truth, and we felt very fortunate to have him on board.

Our friend Russ Terlecki found us two great editors, Cedar Daniels and Peter Demas. We edited the film in a small underground office in Chinatown, where everything cost less. We lived cheaply on fried dumplings that cost two dollars for five and tasted divine. The neighborhood was full of illegal activities, and we'd see daily raids by undercover detectives cracking down on gambling and prostitution rings. In the summer, they screened old black-and-white Chinese Marxist propaganda films in the park.

During the editing process, we relived every moment of our experience. It was like watching a backward roller-coaster ride built with twists and turns that triggered fiery flames. It made us yearn to be back with our Sri Lankan children. When they appeared on the computer screen, I would touch it and smile. The biggest shock, however, came when the tapes were translated. We had no idea what the villagers had been saying at the time. Now we found out that while some of it was beautiful, other parts were unbelievably malicious.

After slaving away fourteen hours a day for a year, interspersed with a few short trips back to Sri Lanka in between, the documentary was finally complete. We called it *The Third Wave*, the nickname for all the volunteers and aid workers who came to help after the first two tsunami waves had destroyed the village.

The film opened in April 2007 at the Tribeca Film Festival in New York to standing ovations and five sold-out screenings. We had finished it only a few days before the festival, so we hadn't had any time to get excited about the big night. Hearing those first and second standing ovations, which went on for over fifteen minutes, was embarrassing and shocking to me. I felt humbled, remembering my suffering tsunami friends. I hoped that many people would see the film, bringing in more aid and volunteers.

The film toured the world after that, with screenings in Sydney, Tokyo, Iran, Monaco, Toronto, Denver, Los Angeles, the United Nations, and all over Asia and the United States. Every time Oscar and I appeared, the question-and-answer sessions went on for hours, and we were thrilled to find people genuinely intrigued about what really went on over there and how they could get involved in volunteering.

In January 2008, while I was on a trip to Hawaii to visit the Pacific Tsunami Warning Center, I received a call from an unknown number. A male voice said he was Sean Penn, the actor, and that he had just watched *The Third Wave*. He loved our film and wanted to help spread the message of volunteerism. I looked into the phone when I realized that it really was Sean Penn's voice on the line. After recovering from my state of shock, I listened to what he had to say. He was going to be president of the Cannes Film Festival that year and asked if he could take our documentary there to show to the world. I told him that sounded like a bloody great plan and rushed upstairs to tell Oscar, who was in bed with walking pneumonia. When I entered his hotel room, by coincidence Oscar was watching the Sean Penn movie *I Am Sam* on television. I said, "Let me tell you about this bloody great plan. . . ."

While preparing *The Third Wave* documentary for the upcoming Cannes Film Festival, I received another call from Sean Penn, who had another bloody good idea. He wanted to take a busload of people across the country, volunteering along the way. We laughed about its being a *Partridge Family*–style bus, where he was Reuben Kincaid and I was Danny Partridge. I hung up the phone excited, thinking it might happen later in the year, and continued with my work on the film.

Ten days later, Sean called to tell me the volunteer bus trip was on—in five days' time. He asked if Oscar and I would come help, and also requested that we videotape the journey. Five days isn't a lot of time to drop Cannes preparations and go on a road trip across America, but my instincts told me to go.

After meeting Sean at Coachella, a three-day annual music festival held near Palm Springs, California, we spent two weeks driving across the country with more than two hundred people between the ages of eighteen and thirty-five, camping out at night and volunteering in different cities during the day. We traveled to Tucson, Arizona, where we went on an AIDS march with the Southern Arizona AIDS Foundation, and to Austin, Texas, where we cleaned up the Barton Springs Greenbelt by picking up trash and removing invasive species, visited an organization that was building "green" houses for low-income families in the area,

Sean Penn talking to the Dirty Hands Caravan volunteers

and attended a pro-immigration May Day rally. At night we'd sing and play music and stay up late talking around the campfire.

Our last stop was New Orleans, where we volunteered with an organization called Common Ground that was made up of young people from all over the country who had put their lives on hold to rebuild New Orleans after it was devastated by Hurricane Katrina. They were headquartered in the middle of the Ninth Ward, the area that was most affected by the hurricane. Nothing could have prepared us for the destruction we saw in the Ninth Ward. There were concrete stairs leading nowhere and empty lots where houses had once stretched for miles. Each lonely stoop was a gravestone for a home. Three years after Katrina, the place was still eerie and sad. It was hard to imagine what it had looked like before the storm.

The local people in the Ninth Ward wanted their lives to return to normal, but since we were there for only a few days, we just did whatever we could. We met a woman whose home had been completely destroyed and had just moved into a new, yellow house—the only one on the block that had been rebuilt. It was a beautiful house but it was surrounded by a sea of mud. She wondered if the volunteers would help her construct a driveway and garden, so we rallied a gang of volunteers to do the job. We set out to build a makeshift pathway from whatever materials we could find in the area. We got our hands and feet dirty and slaved in the hot sun. As the garden came together, the woman said that we were angels sent to her from God.

Other volunteers went off to paint people's houses and log dead trees in different parts of the Ninth Ward. Forrest, one of my favorite volunteers, went to help a woman who had recently returned to her house and had also lost her husband. He had been confined to a wheelchair before the hurricane and survived it, but he had recently succumbed to health problems. She showed the group the water stains left on her house by Katrina. Two miles from the levee, the water had reached nine feet; the scope of the flood was more than any of us could comprehend. Forrest and some others created a stone pathway, landscaped the garden, cleared rotten wood, and painted. The woman brought the volunteers water while they worked and kept saying, "Bless you, bless you, and thank you so much, you don't know how much this means to me!" She was the only one on her street who had returned, and the neighborhood was eerily quiet. Everyone had moist eyes as they worked in silence.

Sean took a busload of volunteers to a massive tent city that had formed under the highway. These were homeless people who had jobs but due to the lack of affordable housing had been forced to camp in the shelter of an overpass. They would wake up and put on nice clothes to go off to work, then return later to sleep in their tents. The volunteers dished out food and sat around speaking with the tent residents, offering words of comfort and just lending an ear. Another group of volunteers went to fix up an old church, and still others moved sheds that had traveled great distances with the floodwaters. A few others rode around on bicycles with a Common Ground worker, helping anyone who looked like he needed a hand.

After the trip with Sean officially ended, a group of seventeen volunteers decided to remain in New Orleans for four more months. In a relatively short time, all the volunteers had begun asking serious questions about the world and their role in it, and many of them felt that they couldn't go back to their normal lives after seeing how much help was needed around the country. I saw that the trip had changed them the way volunteering after 9/11 had changed me. Watching the young volunteers restored my faith in humanity. I saw how even a short trip could make a difference— how a few days spent serving food to homeless people and repainting houses was enough to move the volunteers' lives, and those of the communities they were helping, in a new direction.

The Cannes Film Festival was an extraordinary experience. Sean Penn was present at every film viewing and function. I have never seen anyone work so hard in all my life, and it inspired me to work harder. Bruce and Donny also came, and people swarmed around Donny, asking for his autograph and calling him the real Indiana Jones. When Donny met famous people, he would know that they looked familiar but wouldn't realize that he had seen them in movies, so he'd often ask if they had met previously at the local football club back in Australia. This had us in

Bruce, Oscar, me, and Donny at the Cannes Film Festival

stitches. We watched as Donny approached a confused Woody Harrelson, who seemed to be wondering if Donny was for real. The supermodel Petra Nemcova also offered incredible support for our film, as did many other celebrities, friends, and total strangers.

A few days before our film screened, huge earthquakes struck China, killing more than 100,000 people, and a hurricane also flooded Burma, leaving another 100,000 dead. The new disasters tugged at my sleeves and I wanted to go and help, but I knew it was important to share our message about volunteering with the world. On the day of the screening, Bono and Sean walked the red carpet with us. They had invited the whole Cannes jury to the show. Our film received a standing ovation and worldwide attention. I will always be grateful for the opportunity Sean gave us at Cannes. I will always be grateful for his incredible generosity.

ACT III
HAITI

CHAPTER 14

Oscar and I were practically living in a darkroom in New York City. Although the romance between us had died, we were still very close friends and were working together every day on *The Third Wave* and a documentary about the volunteering trip we'd taken with Sean Pean. Editing the second documentary had dragged on for months longer than we'd anticipated, and I was aching to get back out in the field as a volunteer. We finished mixing the sound and called the film a wrap on January 14, 2010. Literally that same afternoon, I heard my phone beep and picked it up to glance at the text message that had arrived. It was from Sean Penn, and it read: "Haiti??" I wrote back at once: "Yes, let's go!"

A catastrophic 7.0 earthquake had struck the poorest area in the Northern Hemisphere two days earlier, killing a quarter of a million people in Haiti and rendering most of the survivors homeless. Reports were coming in from journalists and aid workers on the ground that conditions in Haiti were horrendous. An estimated 300,000 people had suffered injuries, and yet with an inept government, and the United Nations as well as other NGOs in shambles, the Haitians had limited access to medical care, food, and fresh water. It seemed like a summons from on high—one that I neither could, nor wanted to, ignore.

For the next few days, Sean, Oscar, and I raced around like crazy, Sean in Los Angeles, we in New York City. My primary task was to gather medical professionals to accompany our relief mission. An ER doctor from Manhattan's Metropolitan Hospital had coincidentally friended me on Facebook a few days earlier, asking for my advice on international aid work. He had been all set to go to Guatemala, but when the Haiti quake happened, I wrote to him and said, "You have to join me." He and I both posted to our Facebook pages that we were seeking medical volunteers, and within days we had ten doctors on our team. A couple of them were even Haitian and spoke Creole (Kreyol). My friend Randy Slavin and his mother, Nava, donated thirty boxes of medical supplies, including medications and equipment. Meanwhile, Sean raised half a million dollars from Diana Jenkins, a former Bosnian refugee who has devoted her life to humanitarian causes.

In the wee hours of January 17, Oscar, the doctors, and I set off from New York City in a private jet my fabulous friend Lisa Fox had arranged for us to borrow from the designer Donna Karan. Donna donated not only her plane but also a stretch limo to pick us all up, vials of essential oils, and fifty blankets to keep us warm at night. Lisa's young son gave me twenty dollars to give to "the sad boy" he had seen on CNN.

In Miami, we met up with Sean, his friend the actress Maria Bello, Diana Jenkins, a doctor we called "Dr. Raul," a security

man named Jim McGhin, Captain Barry, who was one of my favorite volunteers from Sri Lanka, and a few others. Sean and
Diana had arrived with a cargo plane loaded with supplies that
people had donated and that they'd had shipped in from around
the world—food, medicine, water, security wire to keep us safe, a
generator, and everything else you could think of that we could
use for a journey to a land where we couldn't count on finding
anything. In addition, Sean arranged for 5,000 water filters to be
transported from China, and they were delivered in just forty-
eight hours.

Because the airport in Haiti was so overloaded and was re-
stricting the number of planes that could come in, Sean had gotten clearance from the U.S. secretary of state for us to land.
Nevertheless, our flight into Port-au-Prince kept getting delayed
by hours. So we decided to take advantage of the extra time to do
more aid supply shopping in Miami. Captain Barry took Sean's
credit card to the nearest Walmart to pick up additional food for
our camp—sugar, canned goods, pasta and sauce, canned tuna,
rice and beans, and other nonperishables that we would need as
a team to survive for the next two weeks. Of course the cashier at
Walmart noticed right away that Barry wasn't Sean Penn, so
Barry had to call Sean and make him come into the store in person. When he got there, they snapped a picture of him and put it
up on the "good customer" wall.

Approximately eight hours later, most of us piled onto a jet for
our flight to Haiti. There wasn't enough room for everyone on
board, so Oscar and Jim rode on the cargo plane, just lying on top
of the goods.

Sean had arranged in advance for the U.S. military's 82nd Airborne division to safeguard our landing in Haiti. The moment
our plane touched ground, their trucks surrounded us. Clearly,

these soldiers were in full control of the situation. When we got
off the plane, we found our Haitian contact, a friend of my friend
Andrea in New York who ran a Mercedes dealership in Port-au-
Prince. When we'd contacted him by cellphone to let him know
what we'd be doing there, he had offered to provide us with a few
trucks as well as several Haitian policemen to serve as our drivers
and security detail. As soon as we'd unloaded our supplies from
the cargo plane onto the transport vehicles, we took off into the
unknown.

It was late afternoon on January 18 by the time we set forth into
the chaotic remains of Port-au-Prince. It was excruciatingly hot
and sticky out. My cargo pants got embarrassingly wet as my
sweat dripped from every pore. We made our way slowly through
the rubble-strewn streets. Dust filled the air and our lungs, making it difficult to breathe. Everywhere I looked, I saw crumbled
buildings and fires. But the worst part of all was the smell: the
sinister stench of the dead mixed with the nauseating odor of
human waste. While many bodies had already been removed
from the streets, there were still corpses all around us, buried
under collapsed buildings or hastily tossed into shallow graves.
Most of the water mains and sewage pipes had ruptured during
the quake, causing human waste to stream down the streets.

As at Ground Zero just after the first tower collapsed, and
in Sri Lanka shortly post-tsunami, people walked around with
shocked, blank expressions on their faces, resembling the damned
in a vintage horror film. The difference between this and New
York City after 9/11, though, was that after nearly a week without
help, many of the Haitians had been reduced to scavenging for
food and water, which they did with the wild desperation of the

dying. The scene also differed significantly from Peraliya because for the most part, the tsunami had killed people by wash-
ing them out to sea. Here in Haiti, all the corpses had remained
on land, and many of the survivors were left with horrific
wounds—deep gashes in their flesh, or crushed limbs dangling
from their torsos by no more than a few tendons. I wanted to leap
out of the truck and start handing out water bottles and cans of
food, wrapping up wounds and giving hugs of comfort, but I
knew from my experience in Sri Lanka that haphazardly distrib-
uting aid under such conditions could easily result in a riot.

Our first order of business was to find a safe place where we
could set up camp, guarded by our locally hired policemen. They
drove us deep into the hills to a place I called "the jungle house."
The large private residence, surrounded by plants, was half-
destroyed, but it had a grassy area out back where we would be
safe from falling buildings and could protect ourselves from po-
tentially dangerous, hostile people in search of food. We put
tarps on the ground to serve as a sleeping area, and I instructed
some of the guys on how to build a latrine in the dirt behind the
bushes, which I had learned from Donny in Peraliya. Sean had
thought to bring a generator, so thankfully we were able to
charge our cellphones, which was critical in keeping our com-
munication lines open. Working into the night, we surrounded
the entire area with the security wire we'd brought. This was the
extent of our base camp at the start of our adventure.

A few things we didn't bring, and wished we had, were tents,
sleeping mats, and sleeping bags. We had assumed that, as in Sri
Lanka, we'd be able to find a guesthouse or two left standing.
What's more, we wanted to save as much room as possible in our
cargo plane for aid and medical supplies. But as soon as we had
ventured out into the streets of Port-au-Prince, we'd realized our

mistake: We knew that we would have no choice but to camp outside, unsheltered. Those blankets that Donna Karan had generously donated were a godsend; without them, we would have had
nothing but the clothes in our backpacks to cover ourselves with
at night.

I cooked pasta for thirty people on a camping stove that
evening and, along with Sean, Jim, Oscar, Maria, Barry, and the
others, came up with a plan. The next day, we would set out with
medical supplies to begin helping people.

It must have been midnight before we got to sleep under the
trees, exhausted and eager to get to work alleviating the suffering
we'd seen all around us that day. But just a few hours later, I was
awakened by beautiful voices wafting through the bushes and
trees. It sounded like an angel chorus from heaven. Although I
couldn't understand what they were saying, I could tell that these
people were praying. Their song was full of a melancholy sense
of love and gratitude, which brought peace to my soul. The next
day, I asked one of our guards what had been going on. He explained that people began waiting in line for food distribution at
a nearby church at 3 a.m., and praised God with their hymns
until dawn to pass the time and ease their hunger.

Early the next day, most of the doctors headed to St. Damien's, a
pediatric hospital on the outskirts of Port-au-Prince, and I went
with them. The buildings were partially broken down, and what
remained was a haphazard array of stretchers and people—
children and adults—lying directly on the ground outside under
a blazing sun. Many people needed immediate amputations or
they would die from their infections. I learned that hundreds of

surgeries were being performed each day. I made it my job to tend to people's wounds, give out love, and assist the doctors. There was no official leadership, so we all just did what we had to do. The medical teams were from all over the world and spoke eight different languages. Somehow we managed, spreading out and covering as much territory as possible. I even saw Mother Teresa's order of nuns there, which fascinated me, as I had admired her my entire life. I kept sneaking looks at them in their white veils trimmed with blue.

On my second day at St. Damien's, I was passing by a grated window when I heard voices calling me to help. Looking in, I saw eight people crammed into a small concrete room. They were holding down a little boy, probably eight years old, whose leg was a mass of swollen, rotting flesh. Spying the electrical saw in one of the doctor's hands, I knew what was about to happen. I found the door and went in to help. After talking briefly, I discovered that they had given the boy some Motrin. That was the most powerful painkiller available.

That moment will be tattooed in my brain forever. All eight of us pushed down on the boy's limbs and held his head still as the doctor sawed off the rotting leg. The boy screamed like someone being tortured. A few of his family members cowered just outside the door, weeping. My heart bled for the young boy, but I tried to stay calm and concentrate on holding him down. I knew that it was either a painful amputation or death for him.

After his leg had been hacked off, the doctors wrapped up his wounds in simple cloth bandages and laid him outside in the grass along with thousands of other patients. Amputations like that were being performed every half hour. At the time, most hospitals had run out of painkillers and had hardly any food or even water to ease people's suffering. I poured out my love and kept repeating the only phrase I knew in French, *"Je t'aime,"* which means "I love you."

We spent two nights at the jungle house, but it wasn't secure. Late on the second evening, a few Haitians tried to sneak into our compound. They knew that we had food and supplies, and they were determined to take what they could, even if they had to resort to violence. Our police bodyguards, along with Sean and Jim, managed to scare the intruders off with guns, but the police confessed to us the next morning that their weapons had no bullets. If the looters returned, we could be hurt or even killed.

In the wee hours of the morning, I was awoken again by angelic singing. At first light, I set off with Oscar, Sean, Maria, and a bodyguard to find the people waiting in line. As we searched, we stumbled across the new home of the U.S. Army 82nd Airborne division, which was on land that belonged to a private golf club called the Club de Pétionville. A ritzy area in the suburbs of Port-au-Prince, Pétionville had suffered significantly less damage than the rest of the city during the quake, in large part due to better construction. When the concrete walls of the private golf club had fallen down, approximately 50,000 to 70,000 displaced Haitians had moved onto the rubble-free grass of the golf course. The area around the clubhouse was easy for the military to secure since it had a helicopter landing and sat high atop a hill overlooking the golf course. When the 82nd Airborne found this location just after the quake, they immediately rented it from the club and set up their operations on the tennis courts. One of the surviving buildings even had a bathroom with a few toilets and shower inside that functioned when the club owner could get water pumped in. It was there at Pétionville Club that we found the people who had sung out in the night.

Sean sat down with Lieutenant Colonel Foster to figure out if we could help. Lieutenant Colonel Foster explained that a small team of DMAT (Disaster Medical Assistance Team) doctors and medics had come with them and had set up a hospital on the hillside. They had hardy cloth tents, stretchers, bags of medical supplies, and had been venturing out to treat the wounded. Nevertheless, Lieutenant Colonel Foster said, they needed more medical help. Since they needed help and we needed their protection, a deal was made. We got our own tennis court to live on in exchange for assisting with the hospital and cooperating with the military in other relief efforts.

The next day, the military showed up at our jungle house with their huge trucks to transport our supplies and us over to Pétionville Club. The volunteers breathed a sigh of relief as we drove through the set of large metal gates guarded by armed U.S. military. After a hot, sweaty day spent moving and arranging our gear, meeting the hospital staff, and setting up a simple kitchen, we lay our blankets out on the tennis court. That night, we slept soundly, knowing that we were safe.

Over the next few days, our camp began to take on a more settled and structured atmosphere. Or so it seemed at the time anyway. Looking back now, I laugh at what a ragtag, makeshift scene it was. The Army gave us several pieces of camouflage drapery to hang over the tennis courts as shelter from the sun. We started to acquire random bits of furniture from the debris: a chair, a table, a few cots, and a bucket for our kitchen. As volunteers came and went, they left their tents behind, so more and more of us had places to sleep and store our gear.

One night I heard a scream from Diana's tent and went running over to her. Seconds later, Sean was there capturing a huge tarantula with his bare hands. It was a Steve-Irwin-the-Crocodile-Hunter moment as Sean carried the frightened critter out into the bush and away from Diana. Most nights, I heard women's heartbreaking screams far off in the darkness of the neighboring town. I knew it wasn't tarantulas they were scared of, but a gang of men who were known to be moving about raping helpless women. The piercing screams would go on for hours. I felt helpless to do anything but pray.

Soon we posted a sign, and Sean arranged for someone to bring baseball caps and T-shirts in with our mission's name on them so that the Army and others could easily identify us as part of J/P HRO, the Jenkins/Penn Haiti Relief Organization.

As soon as we had settled into Pétionville Club, I coordinated with the military to find out how the J/P HRO doctors and I could be of greatest service. The 82nd Airborne agreed to send several armed men and their Hummers out with us to treat people in the tent villages and on the streets of Port-au-Prince, where people lay rotting on the ground, unable to get to hospitals. Each day, our mobile strike team set out at the crack of dawn in Hummers, and then walked miles and miles through the putrid, sewage-filled streets with our heavy backpacks full of medic gear and our military guards surrounding us.

When we found people with heinous infections and sores, we'd clean out the wounds with saline, douse them with disinfectant, and wrap them up in bandages. It was Civil War–type medicine, and often as we worked, a crowd of thirty or forty people would gather closely around, watching the spectacle. The whole time we'd be dripping with sweat and suffocating from the stench.

On a particularly hot day, one of our military escorts saw me swaying back and forth and raced over to catch me before I fainted, then pulled me away from the crowd. He fed me a sort of homemade Gatorade solution—water mixed with salt and sugar, which works wonders as a natural rehydration mechanism—and within minutes I was back in action. The military watched our backs closely and were our guardian angels. Sometimes we'd find people in such fragile condition that we'd take them along with us for the rest of the day until we headed back to camp, where we delivered them to the hospital. Each time we went out, we felt overwhelmed at how big the disaster was and how there weren't enough NGOs on the ground to help.

The Army couldn't afford to use their vehicles to shuttle us about all day because they had important food and water pickups elsewhere around town. So at the end of each long, exhausting day, we'd march back to camp, often five or six miles away, trying to keep up the grueling pace our military guards set. We needed to be back before nightfall because with no electricity or lighting, Port-au-Prince became more dangerous at night. (Even during the day, it could prove hazardous. Sean once got stuck in the middle of an angry mob, and his driver had to use expert maneuvers to escape in reverse down the street.) On the long hike home, the 82nd Airborne would chant military songs to keep us motivated, just like in the movies, which I loved. We'd be on the verge of collapsing by the time we reached the bottom of the hill at Pétionville Golf Club, but we still had an arduous final march straight up the slope to our camp. On the plus side, I lost twelve pounds in the first few weeks and got a great suntan.

Me and the gang after a long day in the field

Taking a cold shower on the days when we had a bit of running water felt like a miracle. Otherwise, we had to make do for
days at a time with wet wipes and some sprinkles of bottled water
to rid ourselves of the stink and sweat.

After approximately two weeks, the military medical team left
Haiti. They had planned to take their large hospital tent and supplies with them, but we begged them to leave those behind. We
were still seeing more than 1,000 patients a day at the hospital,
and the deep wounds and infections we were treating were life-
threatening. Lieutenant Colonel Foster from the 82nd Airborne
agreed with our need for the hospital to remain and immediately
called the White House to get permission for the equipment to
stay. Much to our relief, the orders soon came back from Wash-
ington that the hospital was to be donated to J/P HRO. I was now
in charge of coordinating the hospital and its staff.

On January 26, I was supposed to fly to Australia to receive the prestigious Order of Australia, the country's highest honor for public service, for my work during the tsunami. Instead, I emailed to let them know that I couldn't make it since I was going to continue volunteering in Haiti. I also sent a letter to my parents, which ended up getting published in the Australian press, and then picked up by news services around the world. The letter included the following description:

> Dante would describe it as Hell here. There is no food and water, and hundreds are dying daily. The aid is all bottlenecked and not reaching here. . . . It feels like the job is too big. But good news today: our New York doctors helped evacuate eighteen patients with spinal injuries out to Miami, and we're all so excited.
>
> We are totally self-sufficient with food, gas, and medicines, and a private stash of cash. Sean Penn is here purely as a volunteer and is cutting through bureaucracy to get aid moving and to the people. There is no agenda but to save lives.
>
> Helicopters fly overhead every few minutes, and it feels like the images I've seen of Vietnam. The first night, 50,000 people sung me to sleep, and they sing every night for the world to save them. There is always hope, but she's not here right now.

I'd felt so inspired by the people's singing that first night that I started going to church in the tent village each evening. Sometimes, Sean and the other volunteers would join me. The "church" consisted of nothing more than a grassy clearing on a small rise at the bottom of the hill, where a few musicians played drums,

A little boy waiting in line for water

keyboard, and guitar, and a preacher spoke through a microphone attached to several massive loudspeakers.

The preacher, a wonderful and inspirational man whose real-life name, I kid you not, was Pastor Cyncre (pronounced "Sincere"), spread a message to his people of joy, hope, rebirth, and personal responsibility. The Haitians sang along to the hymns with their eyes closed, faces glowing, and hands raised to the heavens, fervently expressing their devotion to God and prayers for assistance in the recovery effort. Their spirituality was profound and it gave me strength. During one powerful moment, I remember closing my eyes and lifting my hands skyward just like the Haitians, quietly calling for love to engulf and heal us all. I felt at one with the Haitian people.

Even if we weren't attending the church services, we could hear them all the way up in our camp, thanks to the powerful speaker system. Pastor Cyncre would say each night, "Thank you to the Army angels in uniform. Thank you, Sean Penn. Thank you, Alison and Oscar and Captain Barry." Then he'd thank the other NGOs working in our IDP (internally displaced persons) camp: OxFam, Save the Children, and Catholic Relief Services, among others.

Over time, Pastor Cyncre helped tremendously in our efforts. He was the backbone of the village. He registered people as official residents of the camp so that we could ensure an equitable distribution of aid to everyone there. He also organized teams of people to serve as a citizens' patrol, keeping the villagers safe from violent looters and rapists at night. Thanks in large part to Pastor Cyncre, our camp was relatively peaceful, with lower crime rates than other IDP villages around Port-au-Prince.

Late one night while lying in my tent, I wrote this letter to my friends:

> *When I find myself crouched in a narrow passageway of Cité Soleil, the most horrible slum in Haiti, I feel at peace. There is nowhere in the world I would rather be than here. An inch of raw sewage covers the ground, and*

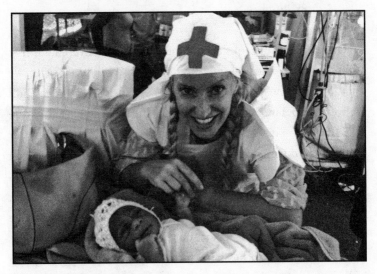

Our 103rd delivery. They named her Alison.

*naked children play in it like it is fresh grass. Pigs sun-
bathe around us as these young ones, infected with worms
and scabies, cuddle me in excitement. I feel like a rock
star, though I have nothing to give them but love.*

*Later, in the clinic, a shy girl with a runny nose and
scabies eating away at her head asks me for water. I pour
a tiny medical cup full of it, and she sits back with a smile,
slowly letting it slide back into her mouth like pudding. I
realize that it is probably the first time she has ever tasted
pure water. I am humbled in my heart as I pour her another cup, and then another. I give her mother a few san-
itary pads, a bar of soap, and a can of milk, and she cries
at her wonderful presents.*

*This is why I stay here. This is humanity, and I'm sit-
ting in the depths of it. In Haiti, you feel alive and in
Haiti, everyone's love is appreciated. In Haiti, it is what's
on the inside that counts and we are all God's treasures.*

xxx Alison

On May 17, four months after the quake, we delivered our first
stillborn baby. She was our first death in childbirth since we
took over the hospital in late January. We'd had 103 successful
deliveries so far. But this baby had already been dead inside
her mother's belly; her skull had been cracked open when her
mother fell during the earthquake. Because most Haitians don't
receive prenatal care—and didn't even before the earthquake—
the mother hadn't known that her fetus had died months before.

In New York, I had often thought of Twitter as a useless waste
of people's time and intellect, but in Haiti it became a valuable
tool. Although I had hesitated to sign up, I ended up using it to
call out to the world for help on a regular basis. One day, we had

a lady dying of rabies, so I sent a tweet out, and within four hours someone had the antidote flown in from the Dominican Republic to save her life. Days later, I was weak and sick in my tent after having vomited all night. When I called out for help from my tent, none of the volunteers around me could hear because the generator was blasting so loudly. So I tweeted my message, and someone alerted Aleda, a volunteer in the tent next to mine, and she raced in to help, which made us both laugh. Another time, when all the hospitals were out of oxygen, we found a fresh supply via Twitter by offering to trade some whiskey for it.

I spent most of my time helping to oversee the hospital, sharing love, and keeping the volunteer medical staff coordinated and happy. I also made regular trips with the mobile clinic out into tent villages across the city, since the people in many camps weren't receiving any medical care at all. The government had

The J/P HRO hospital

declared mobile clinics like ours to be the most effective way of dealing with local health issues. We regularly visited Cité Soleil, a slum that was already in terrible condition before the quake.

After our original team of amazing New York City doctors had left, we formed a partnership with CMAT/IMAT, the Canadian Medical Assistance Team and the International Medical Assistance Team, which would send us about a dozen or more doctors, nurses, and EMTs at a time, who would rotate through J/P HRO every two weeks. They were all hardworking, bright, passionate volunteers who were ready to jump into the fray the moment they touched ground.

Sean Penn continued to work his guts out. I saw him rescuing people, buying X-ray machines for many hospitals, and giving his personal items away. He slept in a small tent alongside the rest of us and ate rice and beans nightly, just like everyone else. He has committed himself to doing this work in Haiti for years.

J/P HRO took the lead as managers of our IDP camp, overseeing OxFam, Catholic Relief Services, Save the Children, and about a dozen other NGOs doing work there. Together, we worked to ensure that the village residents received tarps and tents for shelter, that they had enough food and water, that the latrines were kept up to standard, and that the children had a safe place to hang out during the day. Our camp was the largest in Port-au-Prince, with about 55,000 people visiting it during the day and up to 65,000 people staying over at night.

By May, our primary focus became relocating the village. It was time for us to vacate the Pétionville Golf Club land, not only because it was private property, but also because it would be in the middle of a flood zone as soon as the rainy season began. With the monsoons starting in July, we were in a race against time. Experts told us that the rains would destroy the shoddy,

The Pétionville Golf Club course, where 65,000 displaced people live

pieced-together shelters made from bits of tarp and sheets, which many thousands of Haitians continued to live in. Not only that, but water flowing in rivers through the streets and down the hillsides would turn the land into mud, which would mix with human feces from the ground and cause diarrhea and widespread outbreaks of communicable diseases. Our team began a "Beat the Rain" campaign focused on moving people out of flood zones and providing them with proper tents or even temporary shelters. Evacuating people is a tremendous task, requiring a great deal of planning, but we were fortunate to have military logistics experts helping us.

In Haiti, I saw the same patterns that seem to show up after all disasters: The aid money gets stuck in bureaucracy, the NGOs have meetings upon meetings, small-scale local officials and large governments make increasingly impossible demands, and nothing happens. The good news is that if you can predict what's going to happen, you can seek to avoid it. I had learned from our experience in Sri Lanka, for instance, how devastating the rainy season could be to people already living in fragile conditions, so this time we planned in advance.

After a few months in Haiti, I could already foresee the uprising, the point when people would move out of the shock and sadness phases of their grief and into rage, turning against us. Then, the infighting would begin: the mad jealousy at the neighbors who were lucky enough to get more, the blaming of us aid workers for not doing a better job, even though the Haitian government was doing nothing for its people. In anticipation of that, all I could do was warn the others, steel myself with faith, and reach deeper into my heart for love and forgiveness. I was ready to unconditionally love everyone, even before they'd hurt me.

On our way back from a two-day trip to the coastal town of Jacmel, Oscar, a camp volunteer named Stephen, and I were passing the broken presidential palace when something caught my eye. I saw a professional photographer with a long lens on his camera, and then I noticed small fires burning in the middle of the street. Before I could put two and two together, a group of teenage boys with huge rocks in their hands came running at our car. I saw the whites of one boy's eyes as he sent his rock flying directly at my face. In a split second, the danger registered in my brain and I dove to the floor of the car, covering my head with my hands. Oscar and Stephen did the same. Our driver sped off down the road from a crouched position, struggling to see over the steering wheel as the windows came shattering down around us. He miraculously drove us to the safety of the Plaza Hotel, which was being guarded by two men with machine guns.

Inside the compound, the expressions on our faces must have resembled those of Macaulay Culkin in *Home Alone* after he realizes that his parents have forgotten him. I shook the diamond-like pieces of glass from my clothes and hair and they fell to the floor with the weight of years of distress. The situation had turned dangerous in just a few seconds, and I had felt more vulnerable than I can ever remember feeling. When I walked into the restroom, I saw a girl with nine lives looking out at me from the mirror. I was confused and my ego was hurt, but I should have known better: These sorts of incidents are par for the course in disaster areas, especially after the initial shock of the trauma has worn off. People get angry. Later that night, I learned that the protestors were Haitian students who were upset at their government for its lack of support after the earthquake. I turned on my cell and twittered these words: "For every small crime committed here there are thousands of really great projects going on in Haiti with really good people helping," and in that moment I unconditionally loved the boy who had nearly killed me.

Relocating 5,000 people from our village out of the flood danger zone was exhausting work, with no breaks for weeks, and my toes were perpetually numb. The new land we found for the displaced people was raw, but it flourished daily. A school and market popped up, and soon the village will grow into a city with new homes and the possibility of new beginnings. What I witnessed in Haiti was amazing. Sean had somehow managed to get all the NGOs in our village to work together. I saw how much stronger we all were when we pooled our resources and contacts for the greater good of serving the Haitian people. In all my years of aid work, I had never seen a collaboration like that happen. We sweated and laughed together, and would collapse at the end of an honest day's work.

On a more romantic note, I fell in love with one of the volunteers. He walked into my life looking like a full-bearded explorer and we spent long hours saving Haiti together. He reawakened me to romantic love as we kissed for the first time way past midnight on the helicopter landing overlooking the tent village. It was the first time we'd had a moment alone together since we'd met. Only after we pulled away from each other did we realize that some of the 82nd Airborne paratroopers were positioned forty feet away watching the whole thing with night vision goggles.

Please don't forget Haiti. Just because the earthquake is no longer making headlines, that doesn't mean that the problems have been solved. There's still so much work to be done. We need your help. Time is the most important donation: Come to volunteer, and spread the word through your social networks. Help us to alleviate the suffering. Haiti can be born anew, and we can also learn from the spirituality of the Haitian people. I don't have a lot of impressive skills; I just know how to do a lot of little things that add up. One thing I do know how to do is love. Somewhere out there, a child is waiting for a delivery of your love. Come join us.

EPILOGUE

I have experienced great changes since that tragic day when I Rollerbladed through the streets of New York down to Ground Zero wondering if I could help. Every day on the volunteer journey, I have learned the freeing secrets of life. My parents instilled this knowledge in me throughout my childhood by taking me on their volunteer adventures, but it awakened in me as an adult only over these past ten years when I started doing missions on my own. In between, I indulged in many selfish years of *me, me, me*. Volunteering taught me that life is most enjoyable and satisfying when it is about everyone else. Through volunteering, I finally grew up. At the same time, I learned to be more simple, honest, and childlike.

Volunteering comes from your heart. You don't get paid for it or earn school credits, and nobody forces you to do it. It is about free will and it is a very precious commodity. The leadership positions I found myself in through volunteering have given me inner confidence that tells me I can go out and make changes in the world. When I let go of my fear of what "might happen" or "could happen," my life exploded into what I could achieve, and fulfillment and happiness followed. It gave me the strength to stand up and be heard, to feel that what I had to say was important. Try telling me now that I can't do something and I will find a way around it. A powerful me stands up and screams from the mountaintops, "Hey, the world is really messed up. What can we do to help?"

Saving lives and putting other people's existences back on track used to be the turf of superheroes and comic strip characters, but now we know that anyone can do it. Volunteering can happen anywhere at any time and can last for just an hour. My trips evolved into very long ones because it felt important to me to stay and my life elsewhere seemed irrelevant. I was also having the best time of my life. Volunteering came down to using my common sense and not being bound by rules. These lessons continue to help me daily in every other aspect of my life, from the workplace to relationships.

Volunteering also gave me a deeper passion for and understanding of humankind. It isn't always easy, especially when people don't want to be helped. In Sri Lanka, I endured harsh trials that nearly broke me, but in the end they only made me stronger. They made me feel that the hardest challenges in my life were behind me and that I could take on the world in whatever way I wanted to. I feel passionate in knowing that I am willing to die for some causes that are bigger than myself.

If we could rise above the earth and look down, I think we would see a very dark place. But upon closer inspection of the darkness, we would see millions of shining lights sparkling out from the world. The people who care and show love for one another are these lights, and some burn bright while others stay dim.

Be the brightest light you can be and lead the way in the dark. I feel a real hope for the volunteer movement in the United States and around the world. Let the revolution begin.

WHAT TO KNOW BEFORE YOU GO

Here is a basic packing list and some general tips for preparing for a volunteer trip:

- Before you go, prepay any upcoming bills and leave checks with friends who can pay your bills while you are away. You might end up staying longer than expected.
- Find out if malaria or any other diseases are prevalent in the country you are going to, and get the appropriate vaccinations before you leave.
- Before your trip, Google the area you are going to and print out a few basic maps of the region to take along.
- Pack light. You never know how you might end up having to get around once you arrive—it could be by motorbike, boat, train, on a horse, or by foot—and you won't want to be burdened with an unwieldy suitcase. For the same reason, it helps to have a flexible attitude and a sense of humor.
- Some great organizations to volunteer with, in Haiti and elsewhere, are J/P Haitian Relief Organization (www.JPHRO.org),

GrassRoots United (www.grassrootsunited.org), Global DIRT (www.globaldirt.org), and Youth With a Mission (YWAM.org), but you can also just go with a few friends and create your own volunteer adventure. To apply to become a medical volunteer in disaster zones around the world, visit the International and Canadian Medical Assistance teams at www.imateam.org and www.canadianmedicalteams.org.

- A soft backpack is generally easier to travel with than a hard suitcase. A bag with side compartments is great for stuffing things in on the go and finding small items in a hurry.
- The last thing you want to do is become part of the disaster, so bring your own first aid kit. Ask your local hospital if they will donate a box full of basic medical supplies—they usually will. Also, ask your doctor to give you a good antibiotic in case you get sick or injured. Cipro is a good all-purpose antibiotic. Pack antiseptic, bandages, Band-Aids, and antidiarrhea tablets. (But if you get diarrhea, don't take the tablet right away; you need to flush the bug out of your body first, so wait a day and a half before you take the pill.)
- Bring along water filtration tablets or a water filtration system. Never drink the local water or anything with ice in it—even ice cubes are made from the local tap water and will make you sick.
- Bring along packets of electrolytes (or even little packets of salt and sugar, which are cheaper and work just as well) to empty into your water bottle. Most third-world countries are hot, and it's important to stay hydrated, which doesn't just mean drinking water; you also have to take care to replace the electrolytes that are depleted from your body when you sweat.
- During a disaster there is no time for vanity. Pack basic toi-

letries—unscented cosmetics are best because they won't attract bugs. (The exception, of course, is Chanel No. 5, or any small travel-size bottle of your favorite perfume. You'll want it to dab under your nose to cover up the smell of decay, sewage, trash, and dead bodies.) Leave your hair dryer, curling iron, and bags of makeup at home—but do bring some lipstick and a light foundation with sunscreen in it for day wear. Sunscreen and insect repellent are essential. In the first weeks after a disaster, water is very hard to come by and you might not be able to shower, so bring along wet wipes to clean yourself with. Take a good hair conditioner and a few disposable razors, unless you plan on going au naturel, which many volunteers end up doing. I've never been able to find tampons on any of my trips to a third-world country, so be sure to bring what you'll need. At certain Sri Lankan border crossings, mine were even thought to be bullets!

- Flashlights and batteries are a must. A light that secures on your head is perfect for leaving your hands free when you're working in the dark.

- I've found that the following miscellaneous items always come in handy: glow sticks, waterproof matches, rubber gloves, plastic garbage bags, two walkie-talkies, rope, duct tape, a Swiss Army knife, a watch, and a compass.

- It's hard to know in advance where you will be sleeping, so pack a small tent and a fold-up yoga mat. I've found that light, silk sleeping bags, which fold up into the size of your hand, come in handy and don't take up too much space. If you're going to a country where malaria is a problem, bring along a mosquito net to protect yourself while you sleep.

- You should be able to rely on the local food wherever you are going, but it is always a good idea to take along a decent supply of energy bars to tide you over until you can find something more substantial to eat.

- To make friends fast and to put a smile on a sad child's face, take along stickers, bubbles, pencils, or any other small, cheap toys.
- I recommend bringing the following items of clothing:
  - Two light, long-sleeved tops to protect your skin from sunburn and to wear during religious ceremonies
  - One pair of long pants for walking through jungle areas and for cold nights
  - One light sweater
  - One light, cotton, below-the-knee skirt or a pair of knee-length shorts to wear on scorching-hot days
  - Two pairs of sturdy cotton underwear (no G-strings—they will give you rashes in the heat) and two cotton bras
  - Cotton socks
  - One bathing suit to wear in outdoor showers or for swimming on a day off
  - A pair of flip-flops to wear in the shower and for relaxing
  - Army boots or sturdy walking shoes are a must. You will probably end up walking in the jungle or in mountainous areas. Expect to be wearing your shoes for fifteen hours a day, so invest a little money in them.
- Bring along one piece of nice clothing. You never know when you're going to be rerouted home through Paris or when you'll meet a cute guy or girl and go off for a nice dinner. I always like to pack a little black dress that doesn't take up much space in my suitcase or wrinkle easily. Men should bring along a collared shirt. Many third-world countries have expat bars with strict dress codes that require men to

wear a collared shirt. You will thank me if you're craving a beer.

- Keep camera equipment light. I always bring along a small digital camera with a separate hard drive to store lots of extra photos and a small, handheld video camera with rechargeable batteries that can be plugged into a car.
- Take plenty of cash. You might not be able to find an ATM where you're going. Small bank notes—singles, fives, tens, and twenties—are easy to tip with and use at local markets. Getting change for a fifty or a one-hundred-dollar bill can be problematic. Try to raise some extra cash donations from friends and family before you leave home.
- A small handbook on the local language can be a lifesaver.
- Buy a return air ticket in advance. Remember, if things get too tough you can always go home.
- Don't forget to have faith—in yourself, the universe, God, or whatever you believe in. And leave behind your fear! It's an adventure, so GO FOR IT!

Even if you can't travel to volunteer in a disaster area, there are still many ways to help. Some great organizations to donate to, including several that I am involved with, are:

- We Advance (weadvance.org): A grassroots movement empowering Haitian women to collaborate toward making healthcare a priority, and putting an end to gender-based violence within their communities, run by Maria Bello, Aleda Frishman, and me. Our clinic serves more than two hundred women per day and offers services ranging from gynecological care to the reporting of gender-based violence and referrals for women most at risk.

- The Clinton Foundation: Works to alleviate poverty, improve global health, strengthen economies, and protect the environment by fostering partnerships among governments, businesses, nongovernmental organizations (NGOs), and private citizens. The money Bill Clinton raises trickles down to even the smallest NGOs and actually reaches the people. I am enormously grateful for the generous funding The Clinton Foundation has provided for We Advance.

- Community Tsunami Early-Warning Center (CTEC; communitytsunamiwarning.com): The only tsunami warning center in Sri Lanka, created by Dr. Novil and me after the Asian tsunami disaster. Manned by trained officers twenty-four hours a day, CTEC provides the tsunami victims in Sri Lanka, who continue to live in fear, with a reliable source of information on earthquake activity. CTEC relies on private funding for its existence.

- J/P Haitian Relief Organization (Jphro.org): After the 2010 Haitian earthquake, Sean Penn and I flew to Haiti with a team of doctors. Sean found himself in charge of 65,000 internally displaced people and a field hospital. Sean Penn manages the camp, and all the money donated goes straight to helping the Haitian people.

- Prodevhaiti.org: A Haitian organization concentrating on education and rebuilding schools that were destroyed in the 2010 Haitian earthquake. I know them personally and they are fully committed to their work.

- Boys & Girls Harbor (http://boysandgirlsharbor.net): Founded by Tony Duke, the original volunteer and my hero. The mission of Boys & Girls Harbor is to empower children and their families to become full, productive participants in society through education, cultural enrichment, and social services.

- Claudio Reyna Foundation: Run by Claudio Reyna, the former captain of the U.S. soccer team, the foundation offers free soccer instruction and after-school tutoring for low-income inner-city children. They do beautiful work in Manhattan, Queens, Brooklyn, and New Jersey.
- Global DIRT (Global Disaster Immediate Response Team; Globaldirt.org): Currently dedicates all of its manpower and resources to providing relief to the victims of the 2010 earthquake in Haiti. I have worked with them for over a year and they are real heroes, cutting through red tape and bureaucracy to get help straight to the people.

You can also volunteer any day of the week within your own community. Volunteering can be for ten minutes or a few hours or a day, and it does make a difference in people's lives. To volunteer at home, go to your local American Red Cross, Volunteers of America, or Youth With a Mission chapter.

BRIGHT LIGHTS

I am thankful to the many loving people in my life who have inspired me to write this book:

Oscar Gubernati, for our journey through the very good and trying times. You are a real hero, a loyal friend, and I will always love you. Bruce French and Donny Paterson, my tsunami partners and loving brothers. Keith, Joan, Lyndall, Geoffrey, and Stephen Thompson, my family, who always show me unconditional love and support (and their wives, Jenny and Annie, and their children: Cal, Jessica, Nick, Jai, and Maddy). Jenny, you are a hero to me.

Chris Murphy, my might in shining karma, for your solid friendship and belief in me. Bill Clinton, for his tireless efforts for the tsunami, Haiti, and mankind. Our paths have crossed many times. The money Bill raised did get to Haiti and trickled down to my small work. Thank you.

Laura Yorke, my literary agent and kind friend. Thank you for your friendship and belief in me, and for your inspiring amazing recovery. Carol Mann and her agency, for believing in my story. Cindy Spiegel and Julie Grau at Spiegel & Grau, for their kind trust and vision. MeiMei Fox, an incredible woman, who made me look like a better writer than I am, and for her enlightened spirit. Hana Landes, for her honesty and perseverance in editing the book and her beam of light. Anderson Cooper, my hero who inspired me to go to Sri Lanka.

Tom and Sarah Brokaw, for your support and love in action.

Donna Karan, for your belief in me and for your deep caring heart for others.

Marni Lewis, for your constant love and support and uplifting spirit. You have always been there for me and have always said yes to me. Lola Cohen, my mentor and friend, an incredible lady in such a small package. Sonja Nuttall, a true egoless spirit who puts beauty, love, and others first. Petra Nemcova, a true-life angel who has supported me through her happy-hearts.org fund and introduced the *Third Wave* film to Sean Penn.

Tony Duke, the original volunteer and founder of Boys and Girls Harbor. David Perez, a shelter from the storm. Connie Tarrant, for her grace and love.

Randy Slavin, my American brother, and his incredible family, my other family.

Skylar Casey, my rock and secret angel. Dr. Novil Wijesekara, a humble soul who strives hard for humankind, making this world a better place, Sri Lanka's hero and prince.

Doug Kennedy, for his loyalty and volunteerism, never asking for anything in return. Captain Barry, my favorite volunteer and person on planet earth, who shows a constant kindness and positive energy toward others. Aleda Frishman, one tough, sweet hardworking woman filled with love for women's rights and everyone. You are a remarkable woman. Morgan Spurlock and Jo Amodei, for funding and supporting the *Third Wave* film and for being great men. Dave Pederson and Richard Belfiore, for recognizing the potential of the story and for showing it to Morgan, Jo, and Jeremy. Kym and Callen Anthony, for constant support and raising the money for a new school in Sri Lanka. David Dibo, who traveled in a snowstorm in Michigan to buy me a plane ticket to Sri Lanka. The Honorable Jeyaraj Fernandopulle and his family, the "godfather" to Peraliya village. A good and honest politician who crossed over from politics to become a volunteer and was later assassinated by a suicide bomber. Aung San Suu Kyi, for her struggle against tyranny for freedom and dignity. Dr. Henry Jarecki and Tony Detre, for constant support and air tickets. Michael Mucci and family, for your love and support. Phil Marber, for constant support and friendship. Judy Shipley and Dr. Connors, for their medical support for my missions. David Magdaela, a wonderful human being. Melinda Roy and Taylor Poarch, my other favorite people in the world. Nicole and Courtney Ross, beautiful angels who flew forward to help us.

General Keene and General Trombitas, for excellent command and fatherlike qualities. The U.S. Army 82nd Airborne: Lieutenant Colonel Foster and Lieutenant Colonel McFayden and their men, for excellent leadership and fine gentlemanly qualities. Christine Blood, for her support and inspiring ability to laugh in the darkest of moments. Roshan Waduthantri, my CTEC manager; you are our hero, you never give up in our darkest moments. CTEC officers, my undying support. Jonathan Connors, my dear friend who died in the 9/11 attacks, and all the other people stolen from earth that day. Katie Murphy, my best friend, a constant rock and true support. Hayley Armstrong, for your inspiring hard work, determination, and kind love for others. Sarah Cooley, for the sunshine you bring into everyone's life. Todd Shea, who has carried his volunteering from 9/11 to the tsunami and has never given up on his work in Pakistan. Peter Demas and Cedar Daniels, for editing the *Third Wave* film and for their full support. Larry Buck, for his faith and love for humanity. George Papoutsis, my old landlord who has been like a father to me. Samantha Aezen, who kept the "home base" going while we were away. Sato, always kindness. Warren Buffett, who inspires me through his books to look at the bigger picture. Mary Louise Cole Wood, what a broad you are! With a kind soul. And to all my ladies, Deborah, Monika, Maria, and Shauna. Margaret and Ron Simpson, my other family of whom I am very proud. Julie Santos, for stepping forward without fear. I am so, so proud of you, my crazy rocker angel. Cassidy, for watching my back in Haiti. Michael Taylor, for constant support and faith. Savani, the sweetest and purest girl in the tsunami village. Chief, my Sri Lankan grandfather and comrade. Faine, you are love itself. Andrea Lenier, for stepping forward and coming to Haiti. Stefan, the puppet and human master. Helen Gracie, a safe haven in the storm. To Erika, London, Laura, and Lon, thank you. Pastor Cyncre, a fine man of God, a hero and dear friend. Luciani, you gave me wheels, freedom, and love.

Bill Evans, president of Pétionville Club. You are a gentleman and at all times you tried hard to help and please everyone at a great cost to yourself.

———

To all the volunteers who came and went to all the disasters.

Maria Bello, a sweet, caring, beautiful, intelligent angel, my hero who looked after me in Haiti and continues to do so every day. I love you.

To Sean, you are Haiti's hero, and I unconditionally love you.

Albert Abelardo Gomez. The man I love. Will you marry me?

ABOUT THE AUTHOR

ALISON THOMPSON was born on the outskirts of Sydney in the Australian bush. The daughter of a preacher, she has lived in over forty countries around the world. A former mathematics theorist, teacher, and medic, she has an ongoing passion for camping under the stars in Africa. In 1990 she moved to New York and became an investment banker on Wall Street, later enrolling at NYU film school. Thompson works as a full-time volunteer and is fondly known in Sri Lanka as the "Angel of Galle." She runs CTEC, the only tsunami early-warning center in Sri Lanka. In January 2010, Thompson went with actor Sean Penn and ten doctors to Haiti to help with the earthquake aftermath. They ended up running an internally displaced person camp and field hospital for over 65,000 people. With actress Maria Bello and Aleda Frishman, Thompson founded We Advance, an organization that deals with gender-based violence, protecting the brutally raped women and children of Haiti. In 2010 Thompson was awarded the Order of Australia, the highest civilian medal awarded by Queen Elizabeth II of England for her volunteer work and her contribution to mankind. Her documentary film about volunteering in Sri Lanka after the 2004 tsunami was screened at the 2008 Cannes film festival. For more information about the film, please visit www.thethirdwavemovie.com.